Sweet Dreams, Charlie Brown

Charles M. Schulz

Selected cartoons from
YOU'RE WEIRD, SIR!
Volume 1

CORONET BOOKS
Hodder and Stoughton

PEANUTS Comic Strips by Charles M. Schulz
Copyright © 1950, 1965 by United Feature Syndicate, Inc.
All rights reserved.

First published in the United States of America 1983 by
Ballantine Books
Coronet edition 1984

British Library C.I.P.

Schulz, Charles M.
    Sweet dreams, Charlie Brown.
    I. Title
    741.5'973   PN6728.P4

    ISBN 0–340–35489–5

Printed and bound in Great Britain for
Hodder and Stoughton Paperbacks, a
division of Hodder and Stoughton Ltd.,
Mill Road, Dunton Green, Sevenoaks,
Kent (Editorial Office: 47 Bedford
Square, London, WC1 3DP) by
Cox & Wyman Ltd., Reading

Sweet Dreams, CHARLIE BROWN

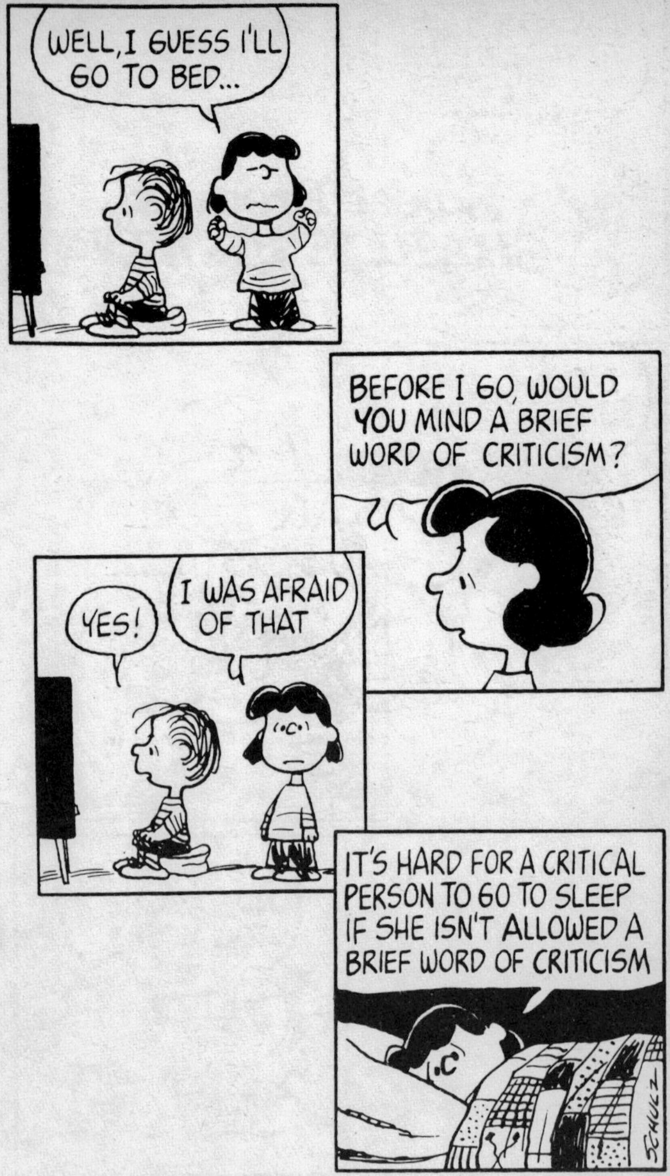
WELL, I GUESS I'LL GO TO BED...
BEFORE I GO, WOULD YOU MIND A BRIEF WORD OF CRITICISM?
YES!
I WAS AFRAID OF THAT
IT'S HARD FOR A CRITICAL PERSON TO GO TO SLEEP IF SHE ISN'T ALLOWED A BRIEF WORD OF CRITICISM
SCHULZ

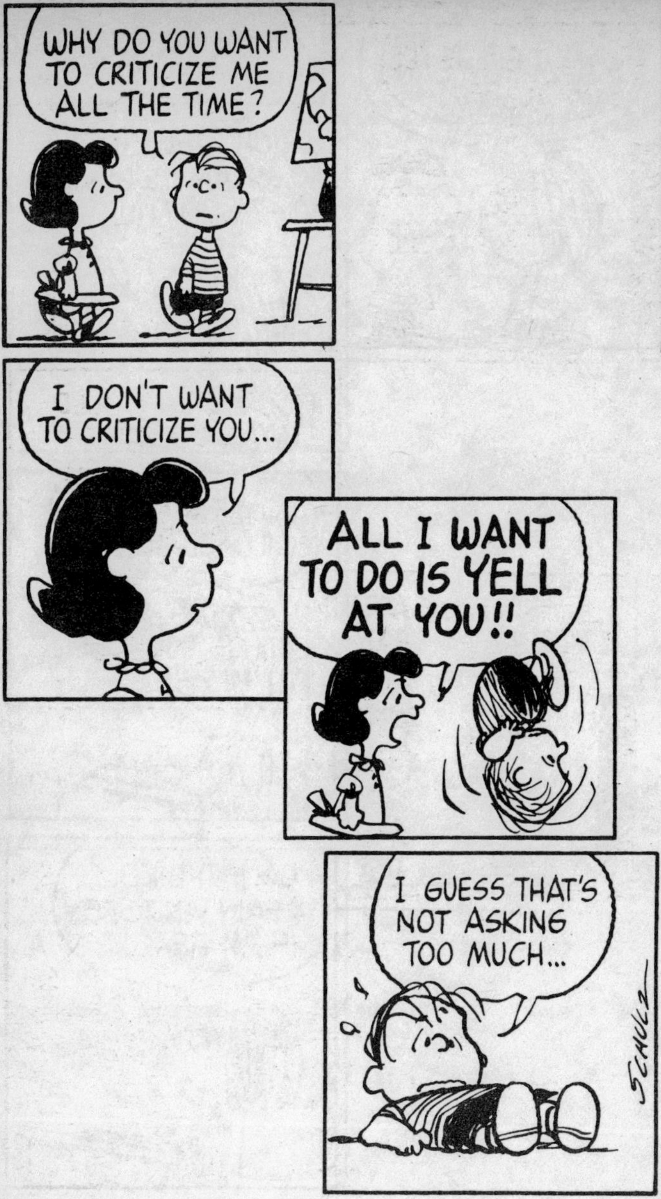
WHY DO YOU WANT TO CRITICIZE ME ALL THE TIME?
I DON'T WANT TO CRITICIZE YOU...
ALL I WANT TO DO IS YELL AT YOU!!
I GUESS THAT'S NOT ASKING TOO MUCH...
SCHULZ

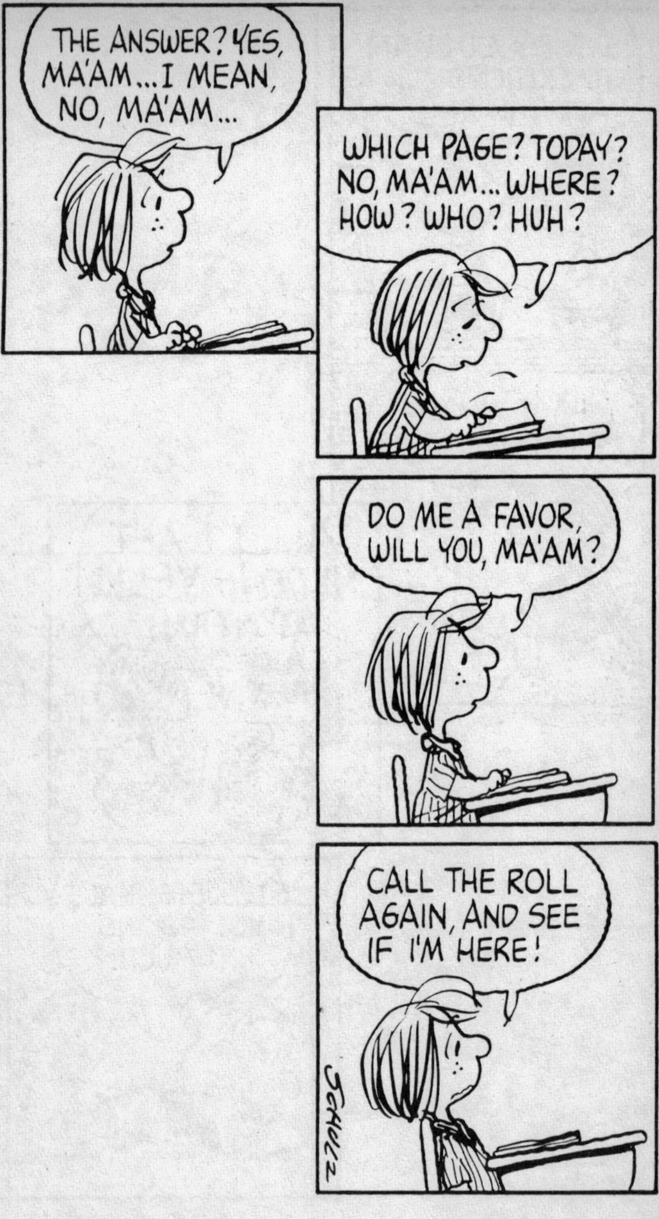
THE ANSWER? YES, MA'AM... I MEAN, NO, MA'AM...
WHICH PAGE? TODAY? NO, MA'AM... WHERE? HOW? WHO? HUH?
DO ME A FAVOR, WILL YOU, MA'AM?
CALL THE ROLL AGAIN, AND SEE IF I'M HERE!
SCHULZ

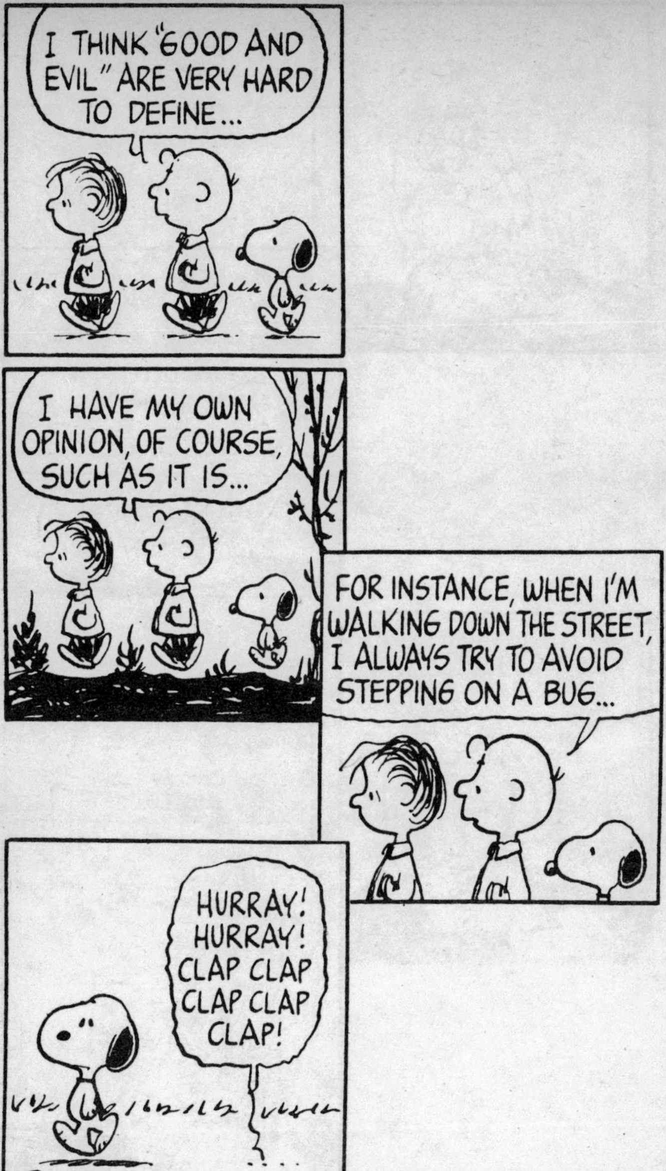
I THINK "GOOD AND EVIL" ARE VERY HARD TO DEFINE...
I HAVE MY OWN OPINION, OF COURSE, SUCH AS IT IS...
FOR INSTANCE, WHEN I'M WALKING DOWN THE STREET, I ALWAYS TRY TO AVOID STEPPING ON A BUG...
HURRAY! HURRAY! CLAP CLAP CLAP CLAP CLAP!
SCHULZ

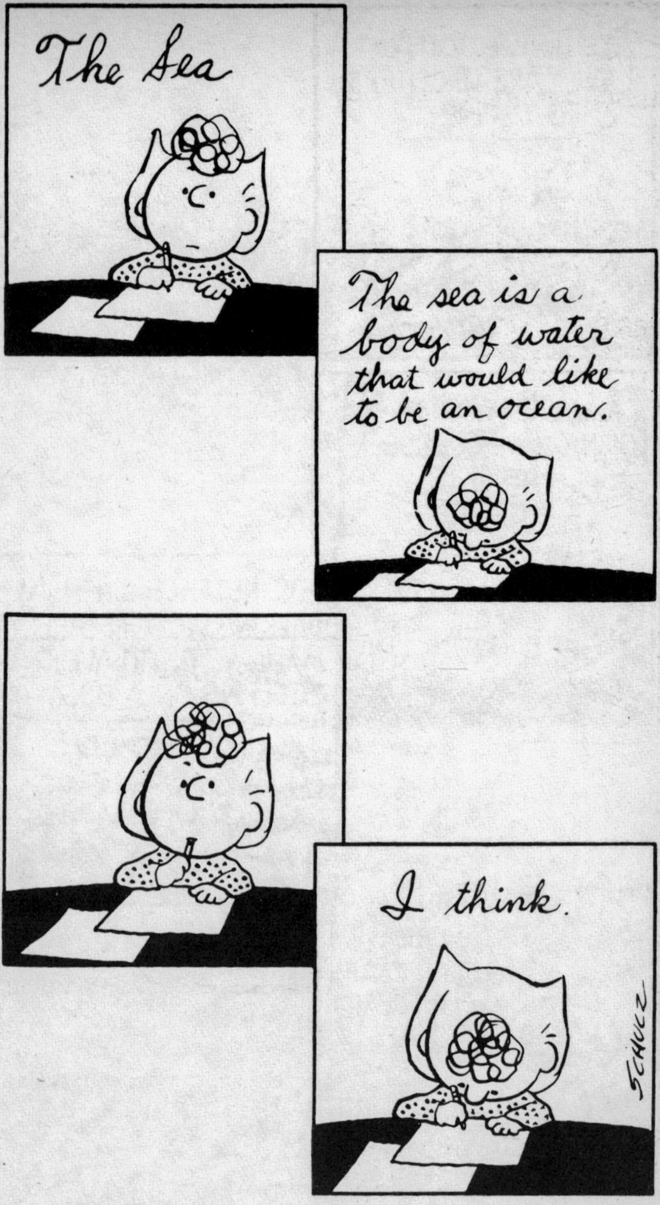
The Sea
The sea is a body of water that would like to be an ocean.
I think.
SCHULZ

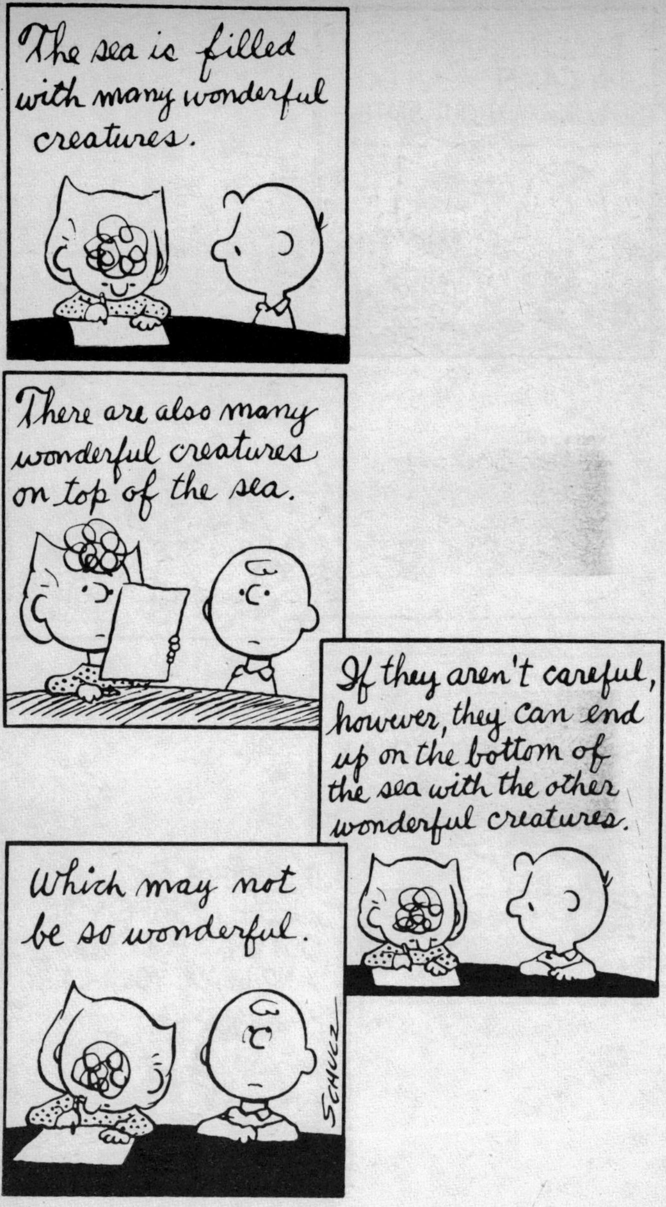
The sea is filled with many wonderful creatures.
There are also many wonderful creatures on top of the sea.
If they aren't careful, however, they can end up on the bottom of the sea with the other wonderful creatures.
Which may not be so wonderful.
SCHULZ

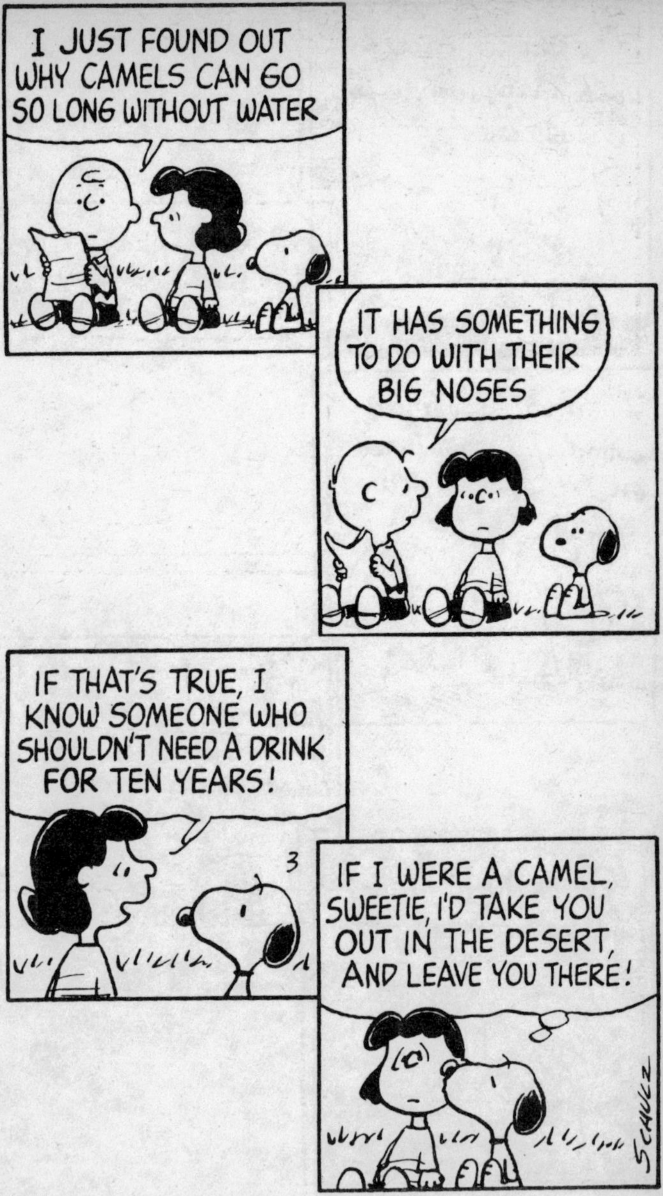
I JUST FOUND OUT WHY CAMELS CAN GO SO LONG WITHOUT WATER
IT HAS SOMETHING TO DO WITH THEIR BIG NOSES
IF THAT'S TRUE, I KNOW SOMEONE WHO SHOULDN'T NEED A DRINK FOR TEN YEARS!
IF I WERE A CAMEL, SWEETIE, I'D TAKE YOU OUT IN THE DESERT, AND LEAVE YOU THERE!
SCHULZ

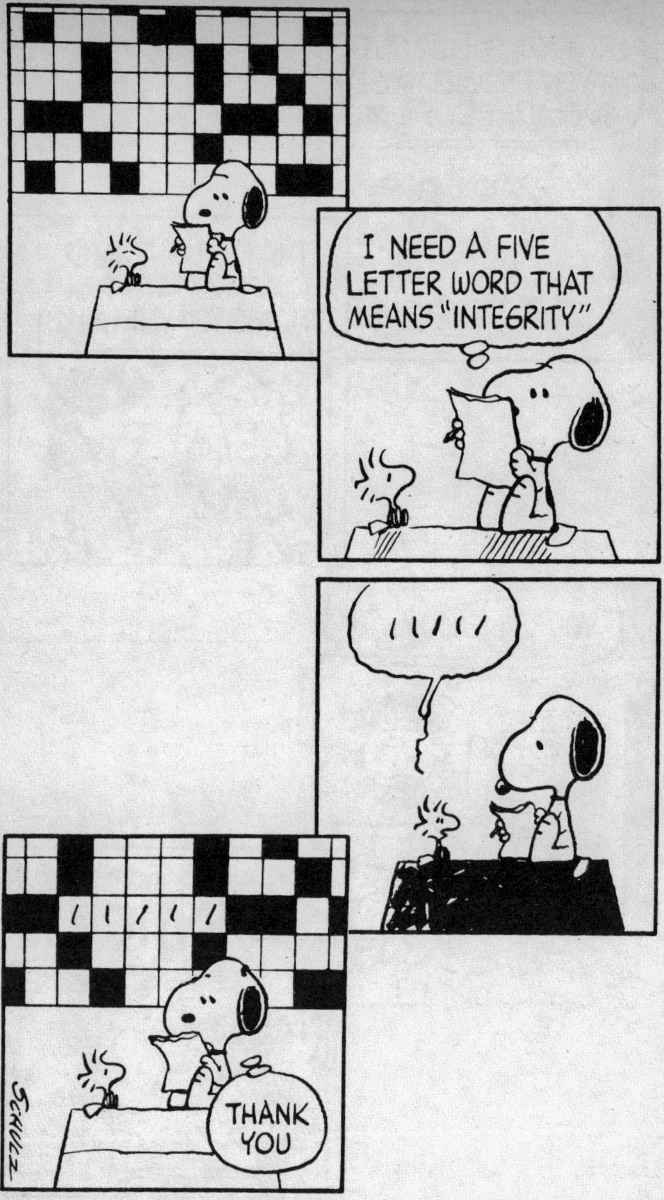
I NEED A FIVE LETTER WORD THAT MEANS "INTEGRITY"
THANK YOU
SCHULZ

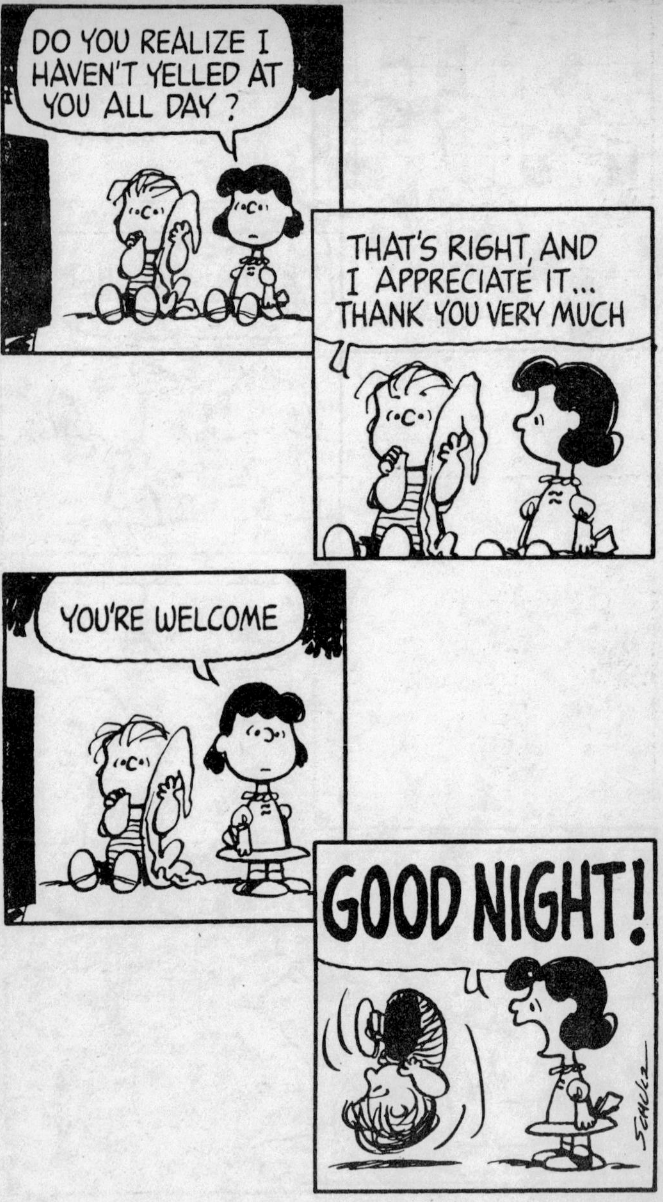
DO YOU REALIZE I HAVEN'T YELLED AT YOU ALL DAY ?
THAT'S RIGHT, AND I APPRECIATE IT... THANK YOU VERY MUCH
YOU'RE WELCOME
GOOD NIGHT!
SCHULZ

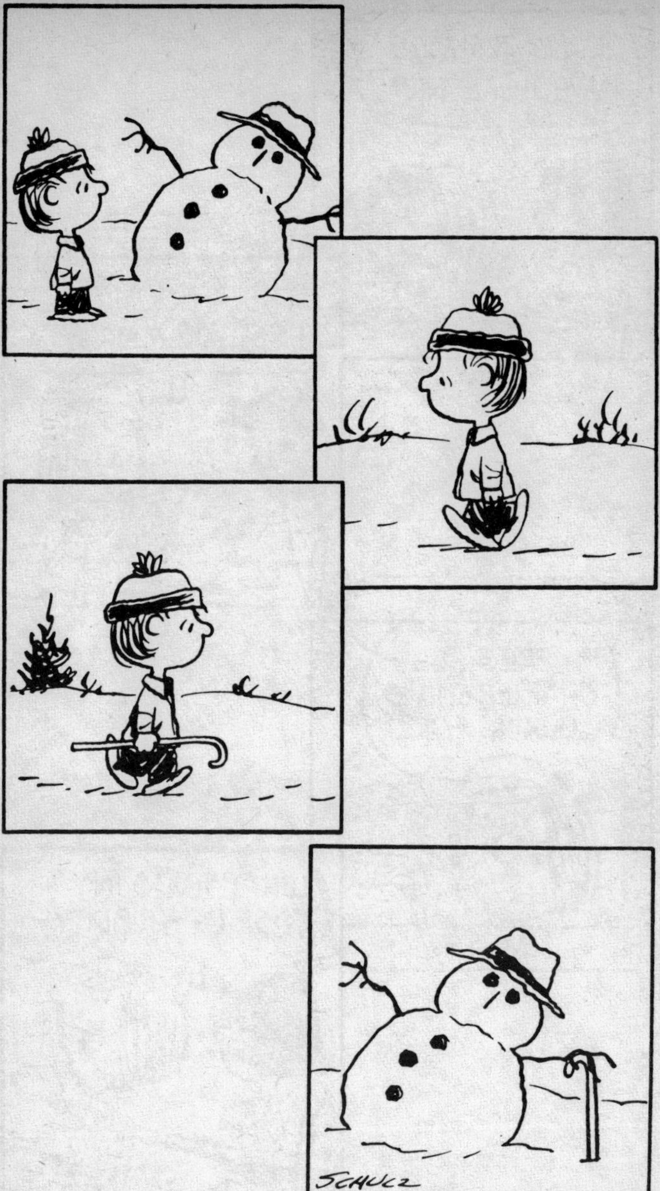
SCHULZ

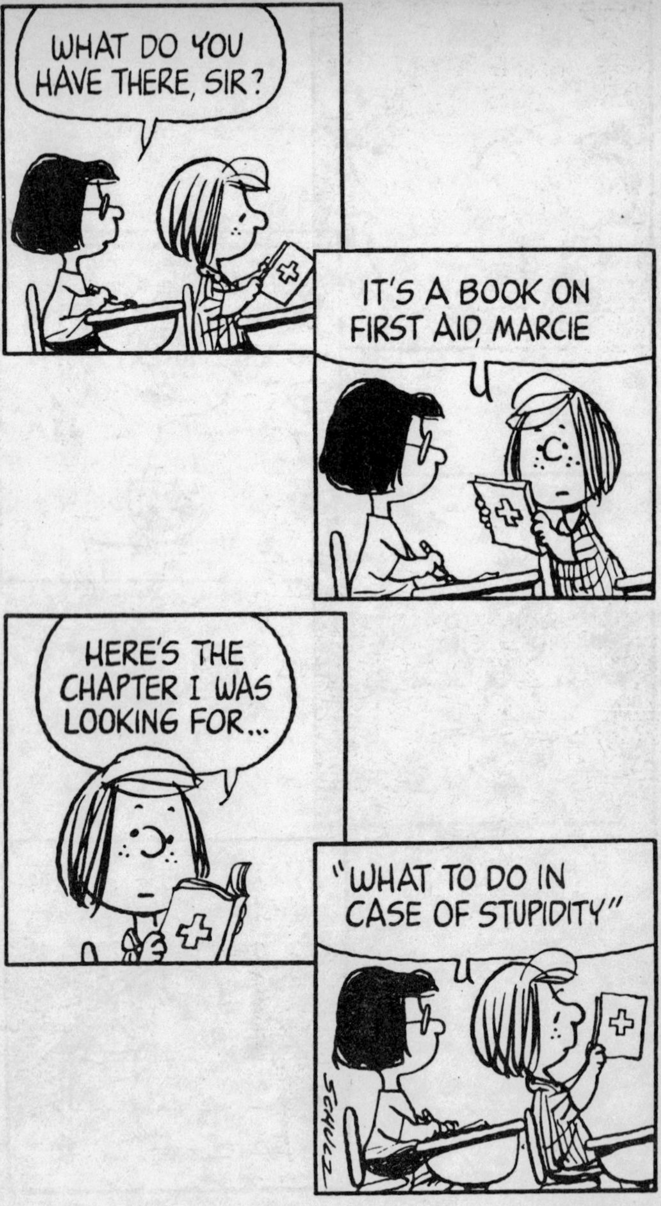
WHAT DO YOU HAVE THERE, SIR?
IT'S A BOOK ON FIRST AID, MARCIE
HERE'S THE CHAPTER I WAS LOOKING FOR...
"WHAT TO DO IN CASE OF STUPIDITY"
SCHULZ

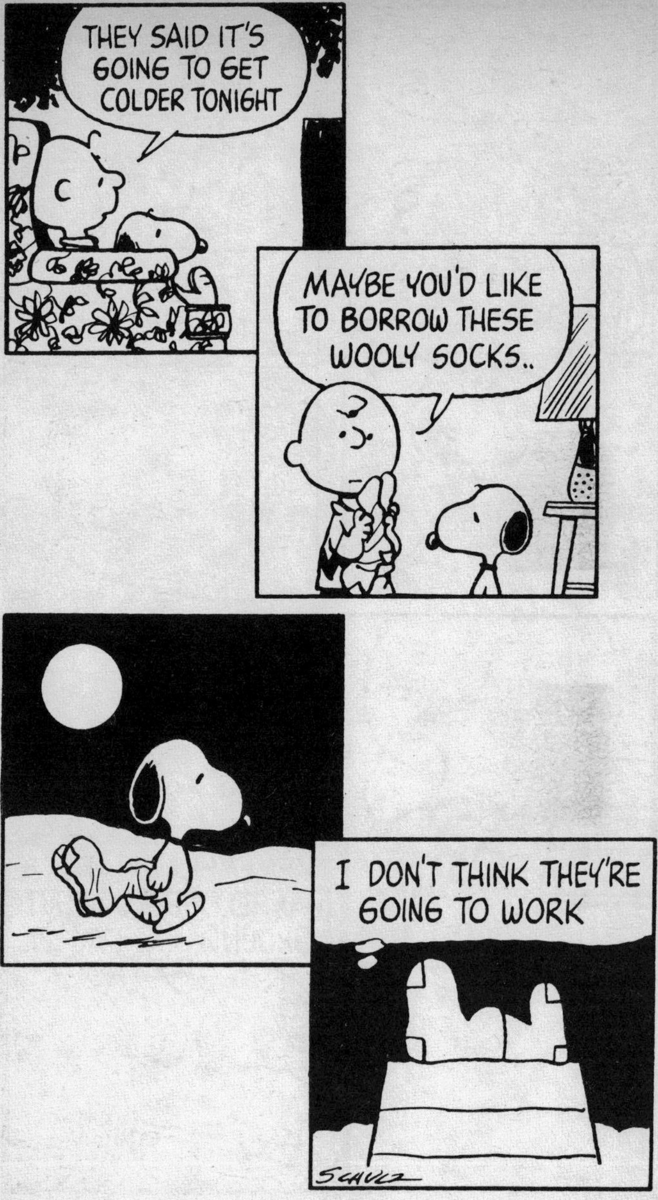
THEY SAID IT'S GOING TO GET COLDER TONIGHT
MAYBE YOU'D LIKE TO BORROW THESE WOOLY SOCKS..
I DON'T THINK THEY'RE GOING TO WORK
SCHULZ

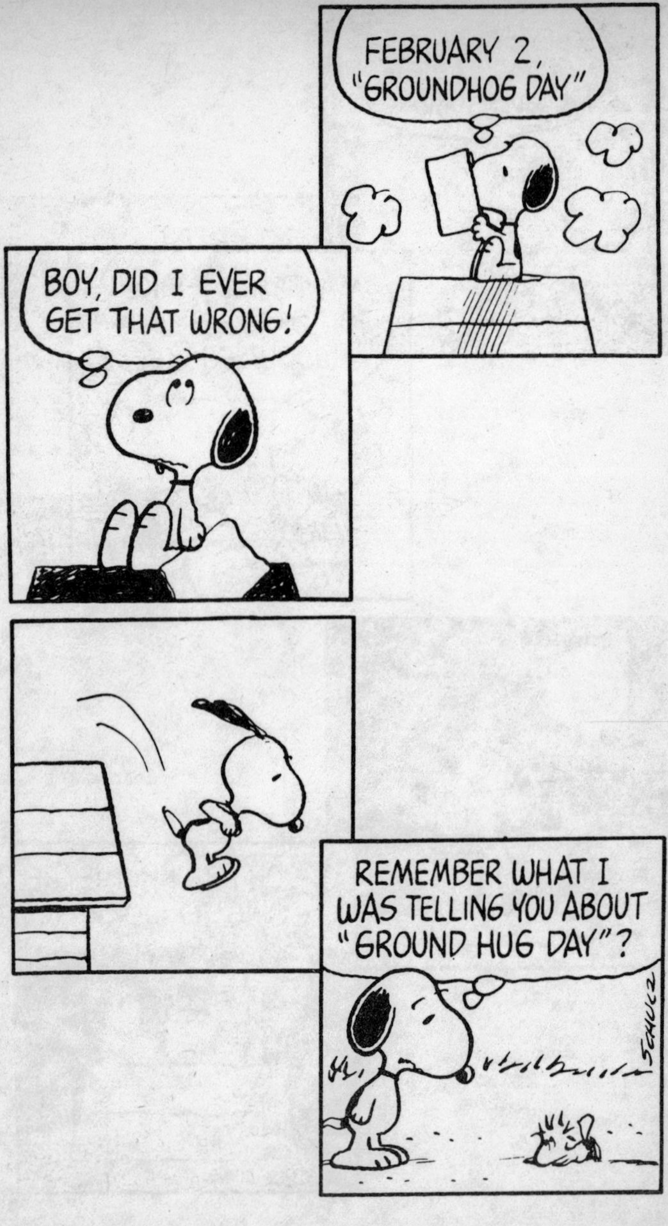
FEBRUARY 2, "GROUNDHOG DAY"
BOY, DID I EVER GET THAT WRONG!
REMEMBER WHAT I WAS TELLING YOU ABOUT "GROUND HUG DAY"?
SCHULZ

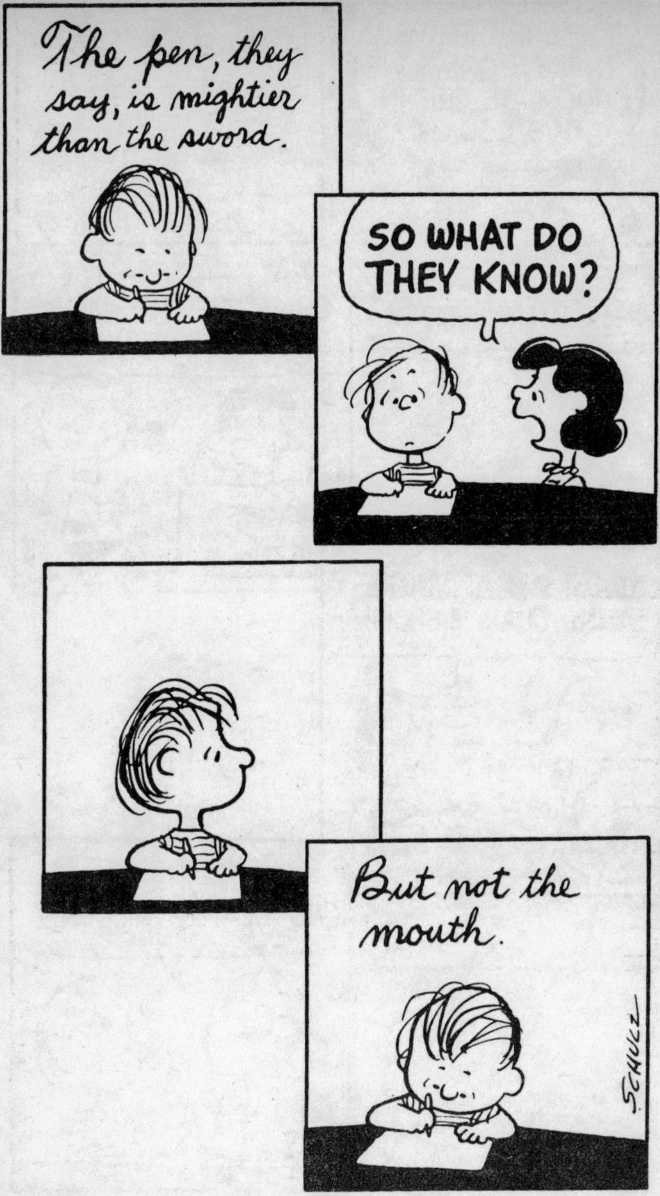
The pen, they say, is mightier than the sword.
SO WHAT DO THEY KNOW?
But not the mouth.
SCHULZ

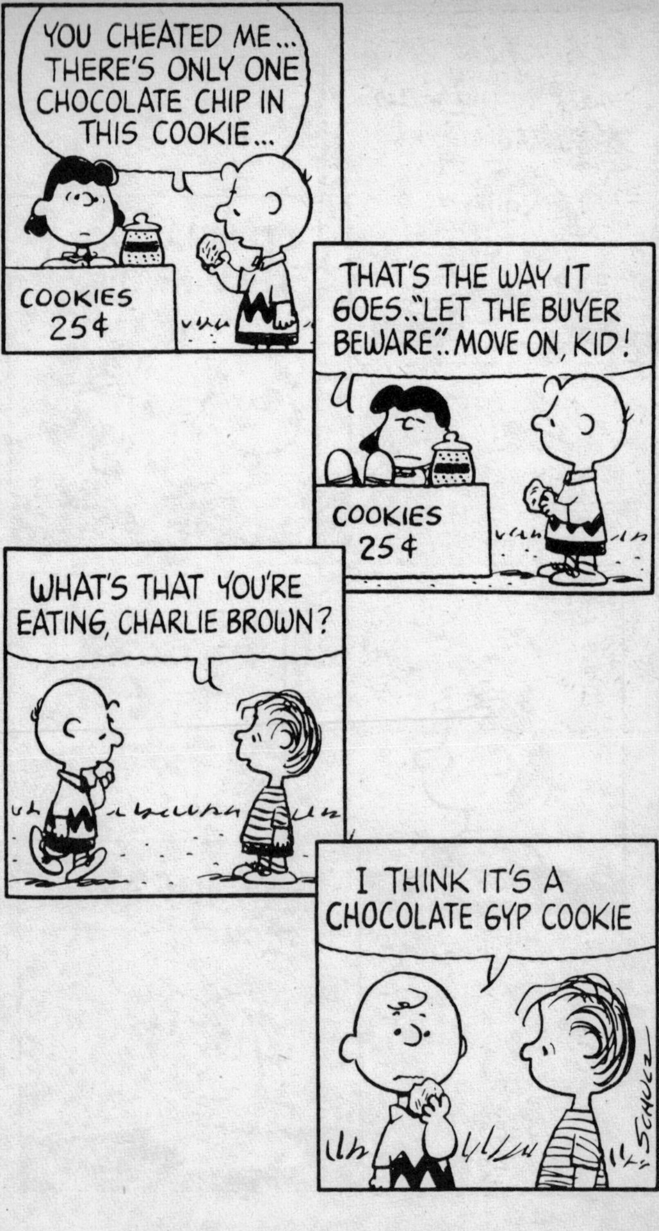
YOU CHEATED ME... THERE'S ONLY ONE CHOCOLATE CHIP IN THIS COOKIE...
COOKIES 25¢
THAT'S THE WAY IT GOES..."LET THE BUYER BEWARE"..MOVE ON, KID!
COOKIES 25¢
WHAT'S THAT YOU'RE EATING, CHARLIE BROWN?
I THINK IT'S A CHOCOLATE GYP COOKIE
SCHULZ

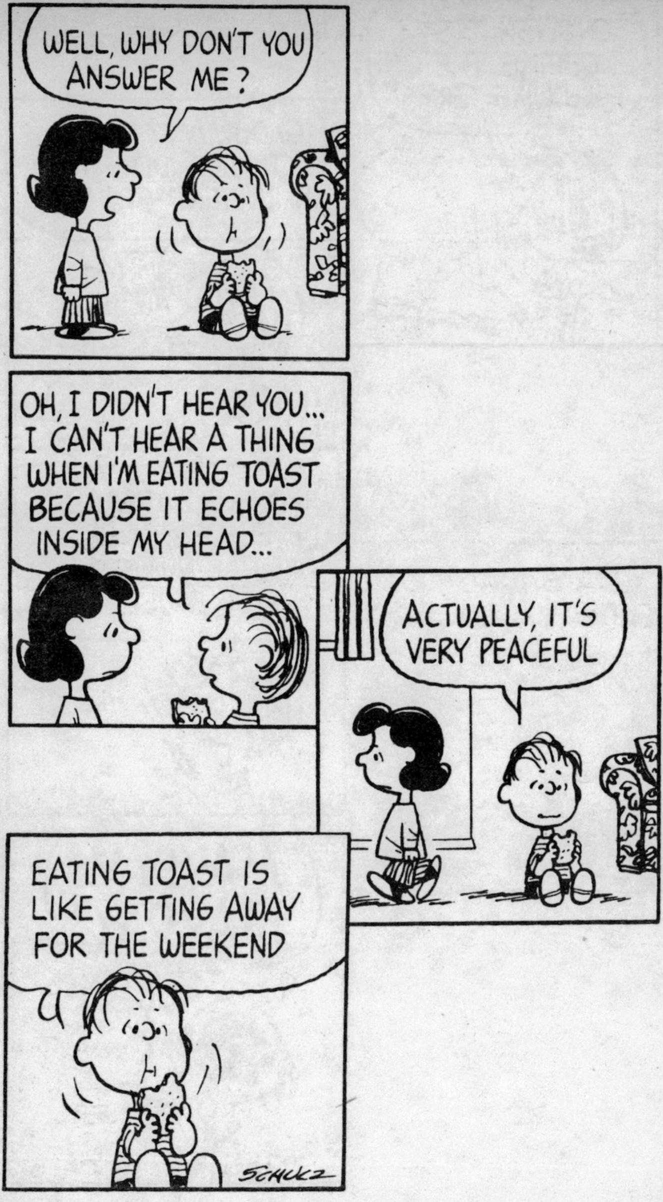
WELL, WHY DON'T YOU ANSWER ME?
OH, I DIDN'T HEAR YOU... I CAN'T HEAR A THING WHEN I'M EATING TOAST BECAUSE IT ECHOES INSIDE MY HEAD...
ACTUALLY, IT'S VERY PEACEFUL
EATING TOAST IS LIKE GETTING AWAY FOR THE WEEKEND
SCHULZ

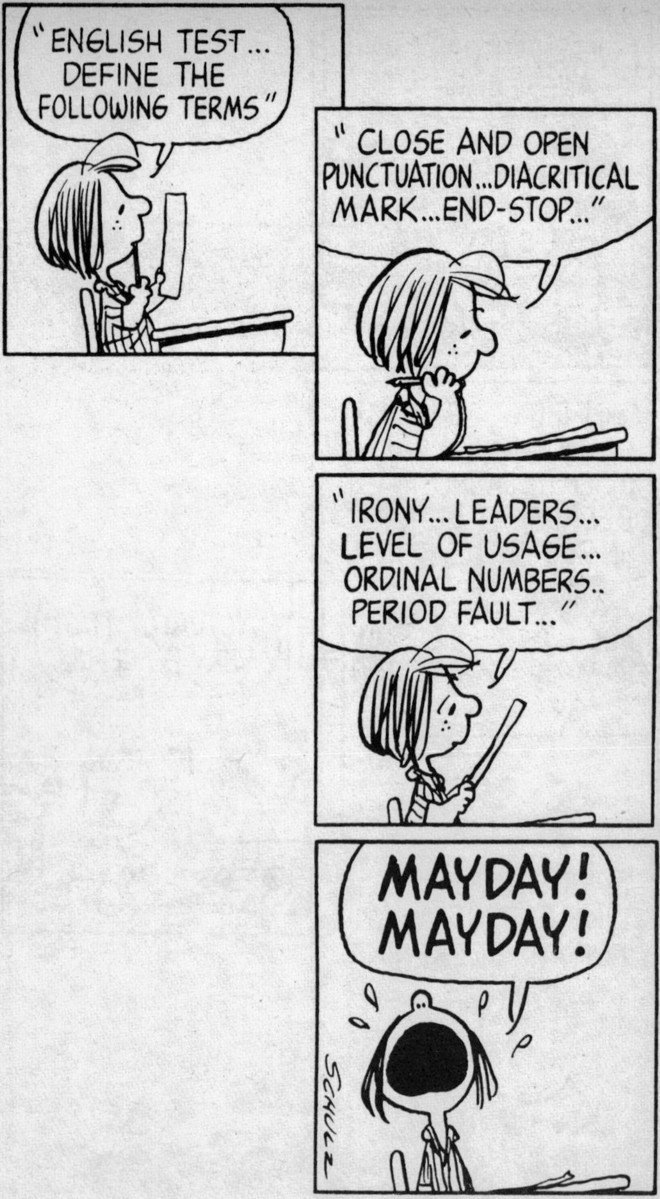
"ENGLISH TEST... DEFINE THE FOLLOWING TERMS"
"CLOSE AND OPEN PUNCTUATION...DIACRITICAL MARK...END-STOP..."
"IRONY... LEADERS... LEVEL OF USAGE... ORDINAL NUMBERS.. PERIOD FAULT..."
MAYDAY! MAYDAY!
SCHULZ

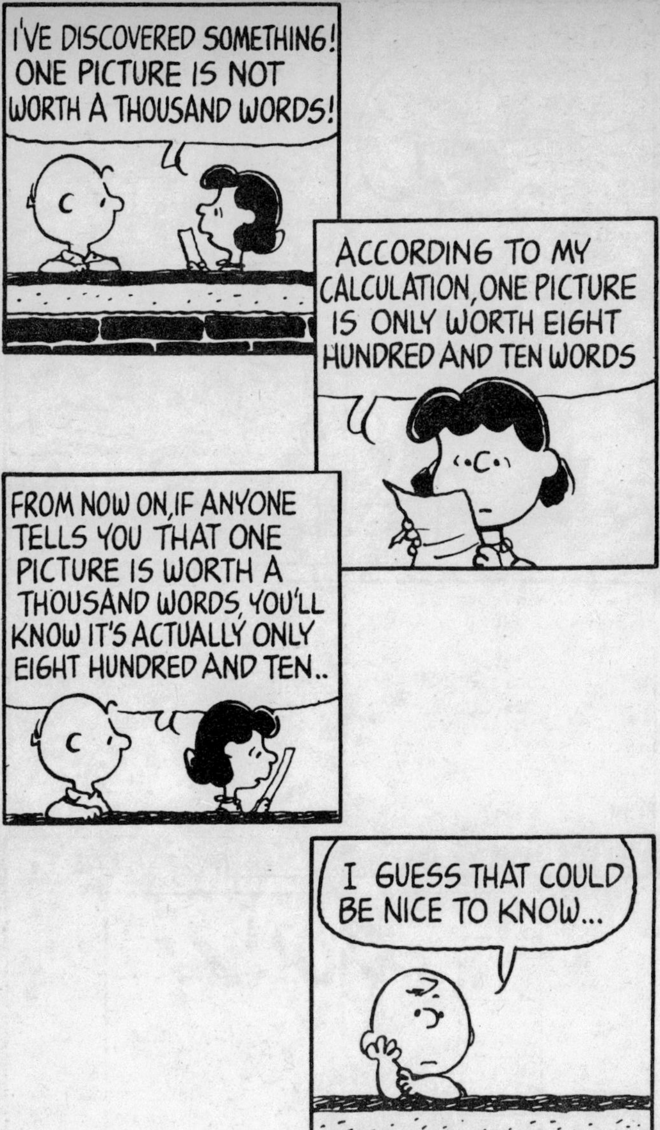
I'VE DISCOVERED SOMETHING! ONE PICTURE IS NOT WORTH A THOUSAND WORDS!
ACCORDING TO MY CALCULATION, ONE PICTURE IS ONLY WORTH EIGHT HUNDRED AND TEN WORDS
FROM NOW ON, IF ANYONE TELLS YOU THAT ONE PICTURE IS WORTH A THOUSAND WORDS, YOU'LL KNOW IT'S ACTUALLY ONLY EIGHT HUNDRED AND TEN..
I GUESS THAT COULD BE NICE TO KNOW...

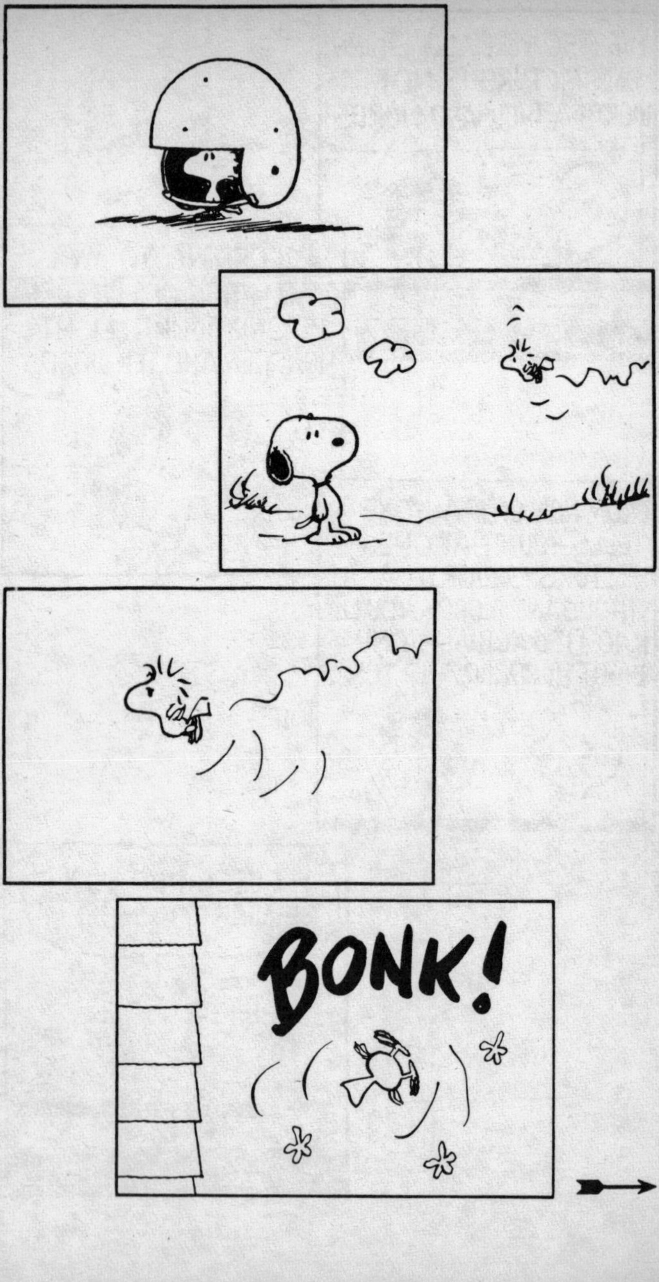
BONK!

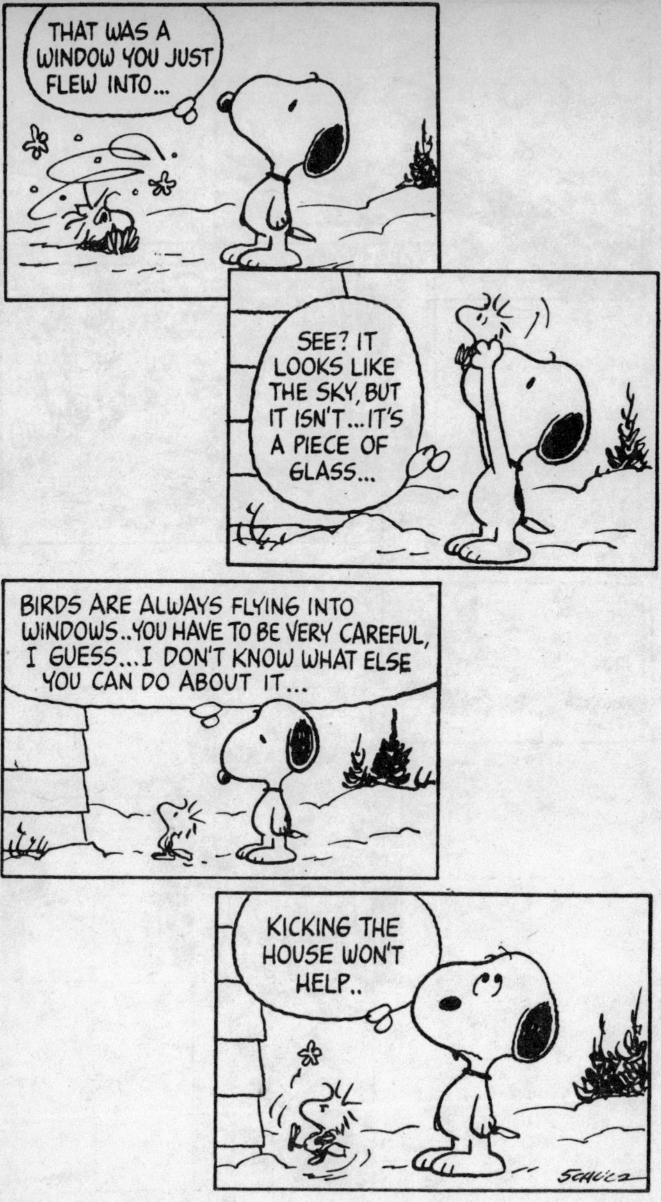
THAT WAS A WINDOW YOU JUST FLEW INTO...
SEE? IT LOOKS LIKE THE SKY, BUT IT ISN'T...IT'S A PIECE OF GLASS...
BIRDS ARE ALWAYS FLYING INTO WINDOWS..YOU HAVE TO BE VERY CAREFUL, I GUESS...I DON'T KNOW WHAT ELSE YOU CAN DO ABOUT IT...
KICKING THE HOUSE WON'T HELP..
SCHULZ

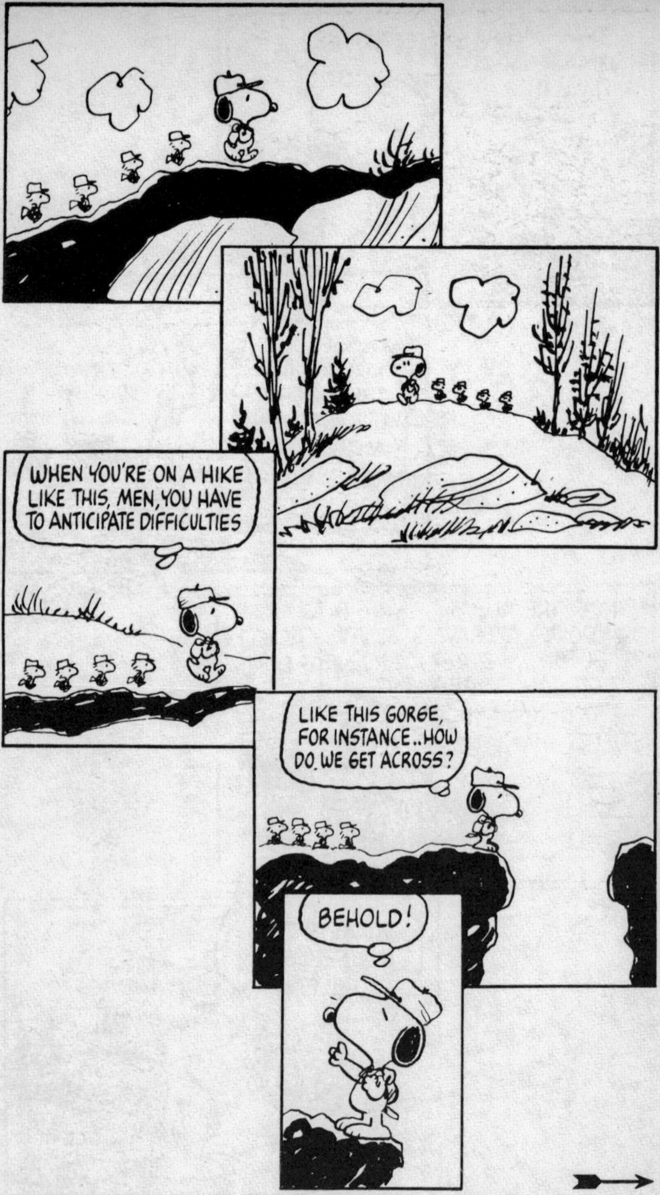
WHEN YOU'RE ON A HIKE LIKE THIS, MEN, YOU HAVE TO ANTICIPATE DIFFICULTIES
LIKE THIS GORGE, FOR INSTANCE..HOW DO WE GET ACROSS?
BEHOLD!

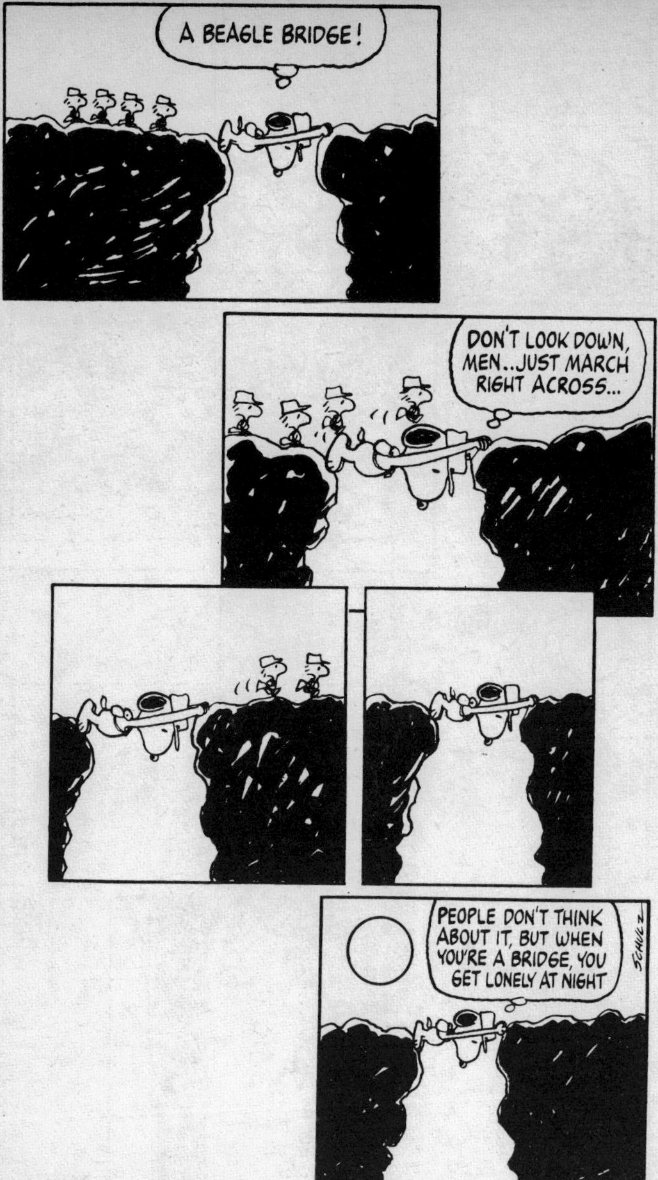
A BEAGLE BRIDGE!
DON'T LOOK DOWN, MEN..JUST MARCH RIGHT ACROSS...
PEOPLE DON'T THINK ABOUT IT, BUT WHEN YOU'RE A BRIDGE, YOU GET LONELY AT NIGHT
SCHULZ

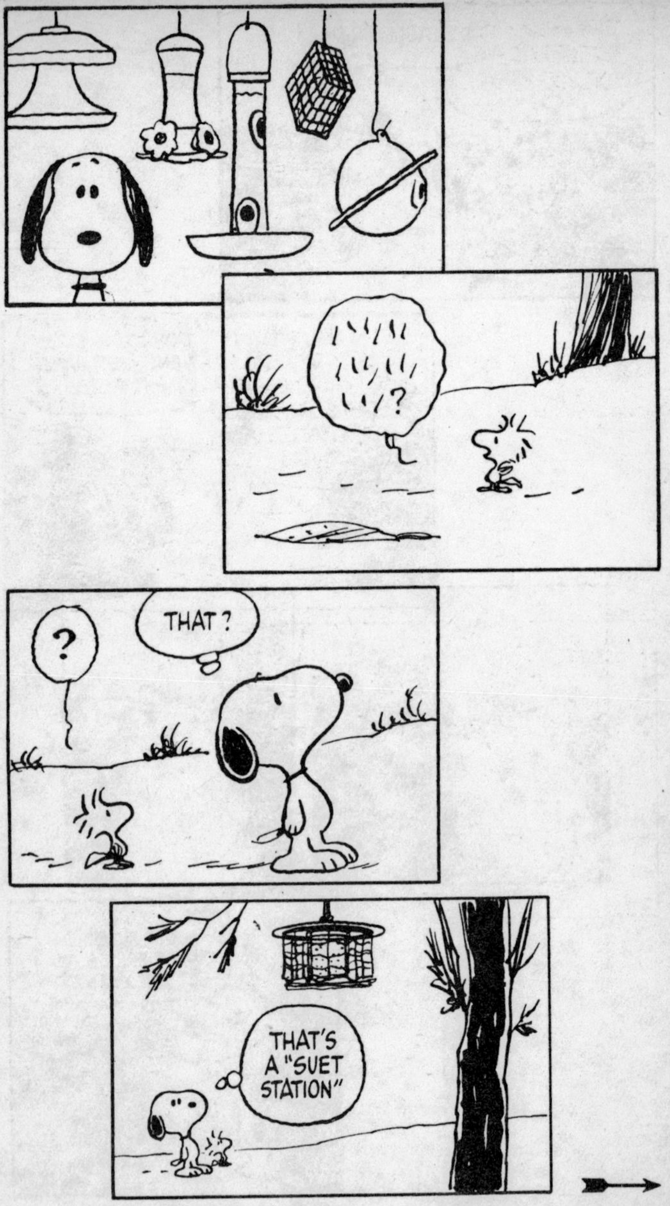

?
?
THAT?
THAT'S A "SUET STATION"

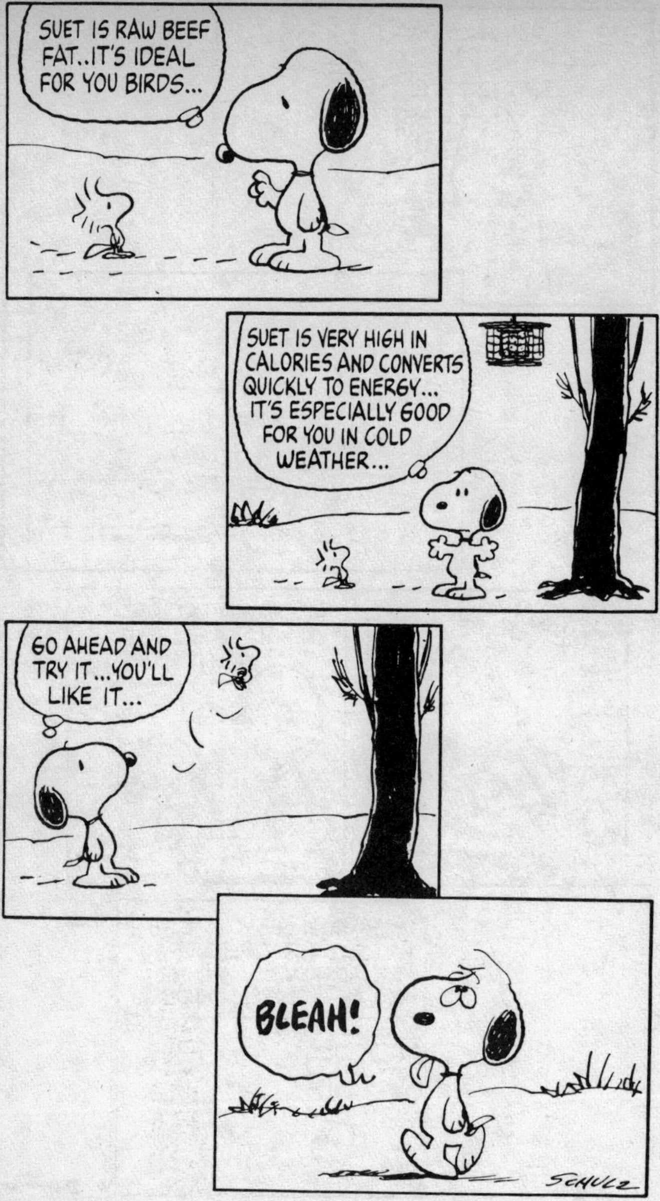
SUET IS RAW BEEF FAT..IT'S IDEAL FOR YOU BIRDS...
SUET IS VERY HIGH IN CALORIES AND CONVERTS QUICKLY TO ENERGY... IT'S ESPECIALLY GOOD FOR YOU IN COLD WEATHER...
GO AHEAD AND TRY IT...YOU'LL LIKE IT...
BLEAH!
SCHULZ

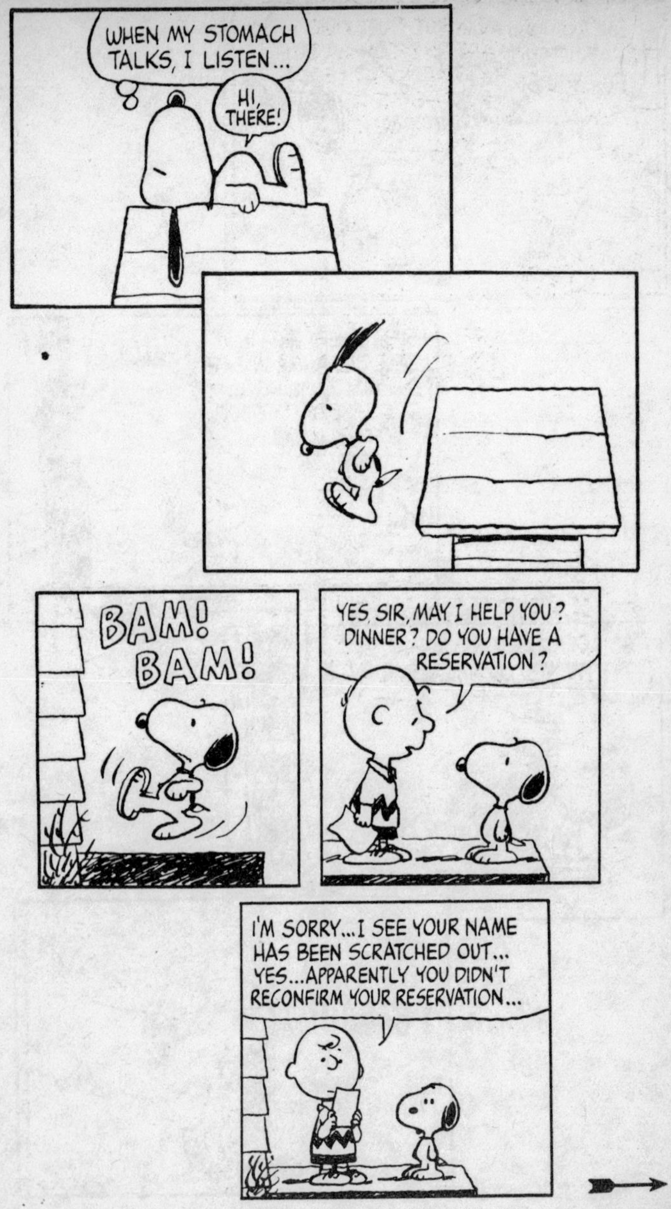
WHEN MY STOMACH TALKS, I LISTEN...
HI, THERE!
BAM! BAM!
YES, SIR, MAY I HELP YOU? DINNER? DO YOU HAVE A RESERVATION?
I'M SORRY...I SEE YOUR NAME HAS BEEN SCRATCHED OUT... YES...APPARENTLY YOU DIDN'T RECONFIRM YOUR RESERVATION...

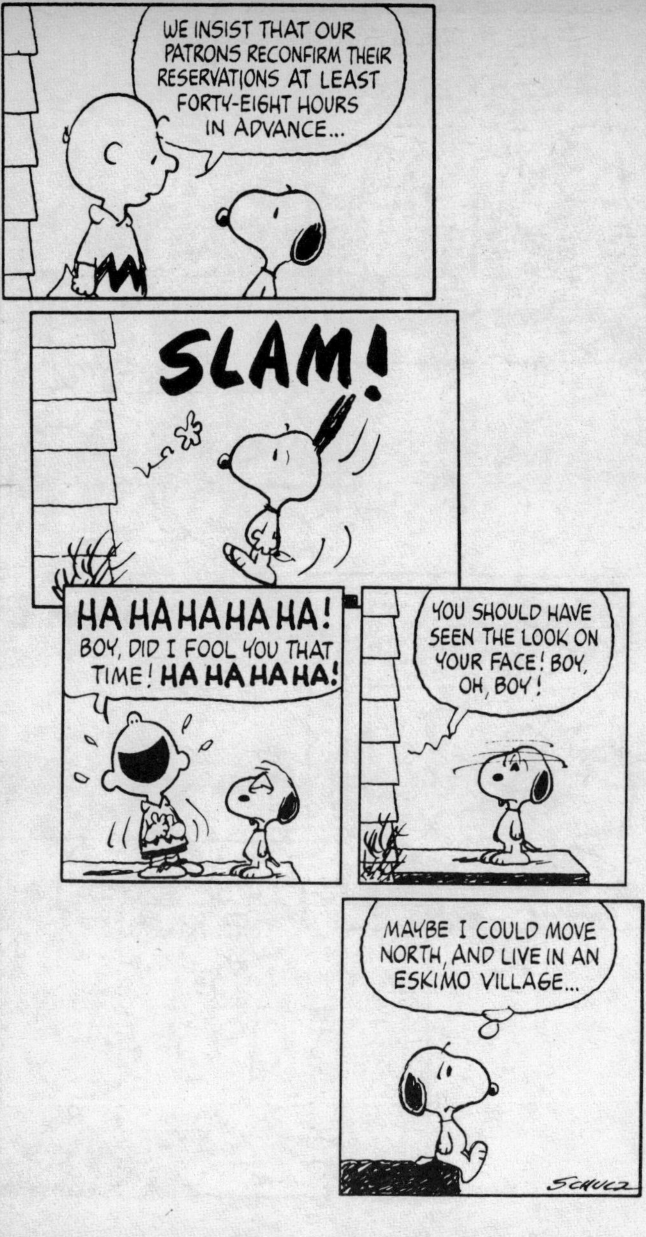
WE INSIST THAT OUR PATRONS RECONFIRM THEIR RESERVATIONS AT LEAST FORTY-EIGHT HOURS IN ADVANCE...
SLAM!
HA HA HA HA HA HA! BOY, DID I FOOL YOU THAT TIME! HA HA HA HA HA!
YOU SHOULD HAVE SEEN THE LOOK ON YOUR FACE! BOY, OH, BOY!
MAYBE I COULD MOVE NORTH, AND LIVE IN AN ESKIMO VILLAGE...
SCHULZ

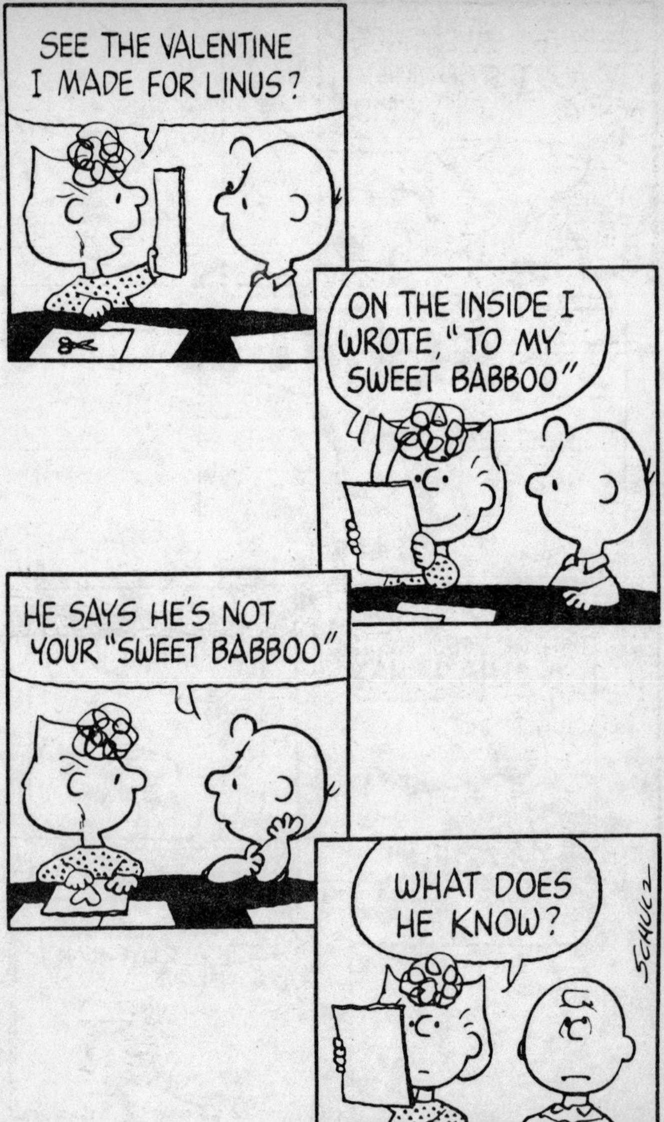
SEE THE VALENTINE I MADE FOR LINUS?
ON THE INSIDE I WROTE, "TO MY SWEET BABBOO"
HE SAYS HE'S NOT YOUR "SWEET BABBOO"
WHAT DOES HE KNOW?
SCHULZ

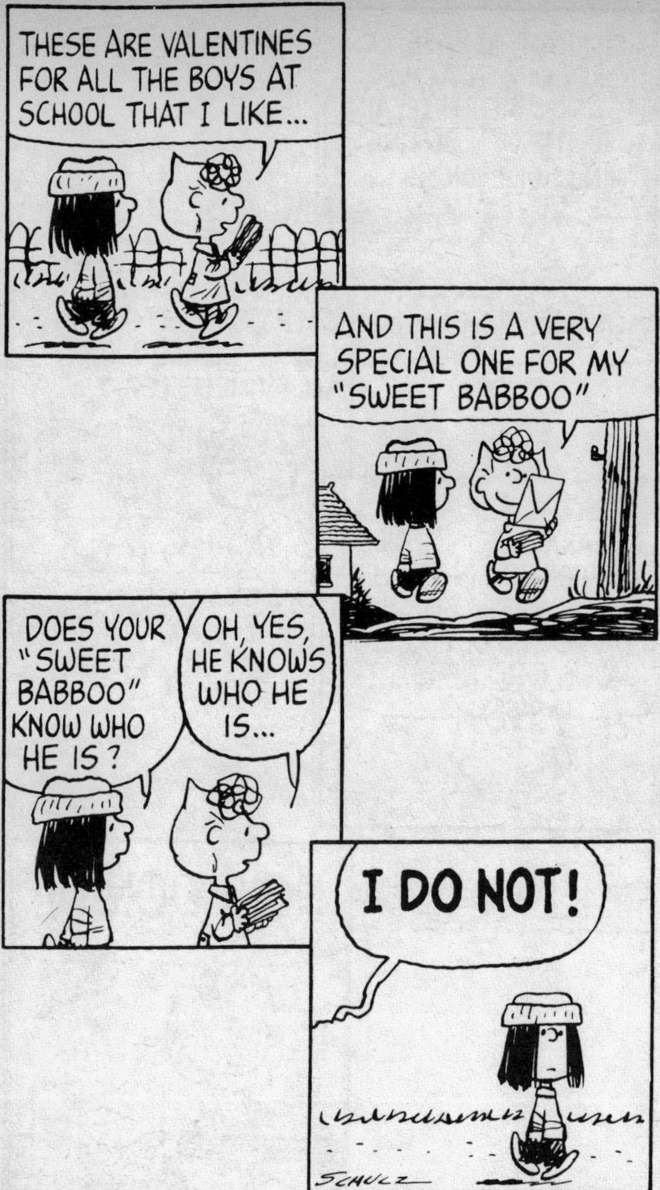
THESE ARE VALENTINES FOR ALL THE BOYS AT SCHOOL THAT I LIKE...
AND THIS IS A VERY SPECIAL ONE FOR MY "SWEET BABBOO"
DOES YOUR "SWEET BABBOO" KNOW WHO HE IS?
OH, YES, HE KNOWS WHO HE IS...
I DO NOT!
SCHULZ

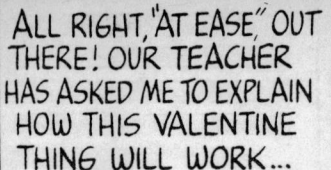

ALL RIGHT, "AT EASE" OUT THERE! OUR TEACHER HAS ASKED ME TO EXPLAIN HOW THIS VALENTINE THING WILL WORK...

EACH STUDENT WILL DROP HIS OR HER VALENTINE INTO THIS BOX...PLEASE WRITE ALL NAMES CLEARLY...

SPECIAL TERMS OF ENDEARMENT LIKE "SWEET BABBOO," FOR INSTANCE, ARE PERMITTED BECAUSE THAT PERSON OBVIOUSLY KNOWS WHO HE IS...

NO, I DON'T!!

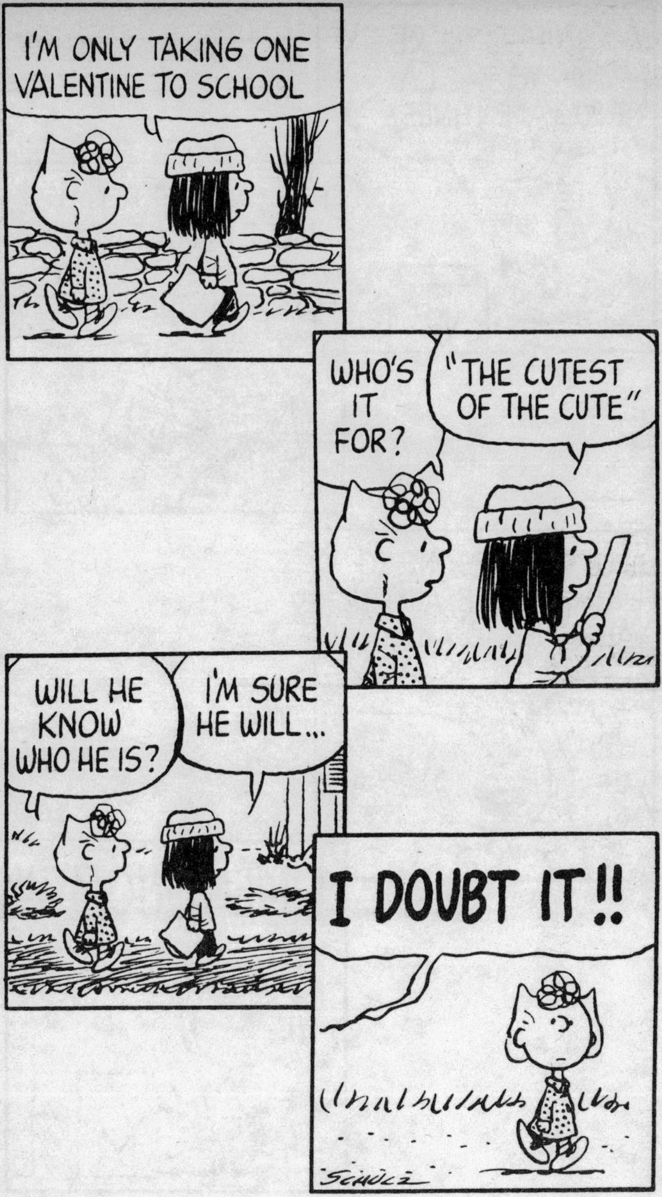
I'M ONLY TAKING ONE VALENTINE TO SCHOOL
WHO'S IT FOR?
"THE CUTEST OF THE CUTE"
WILL HE KNOW WHO HE IS?
I'M SURE HE WILL...
I DOUBT IT!!
SCHULZ

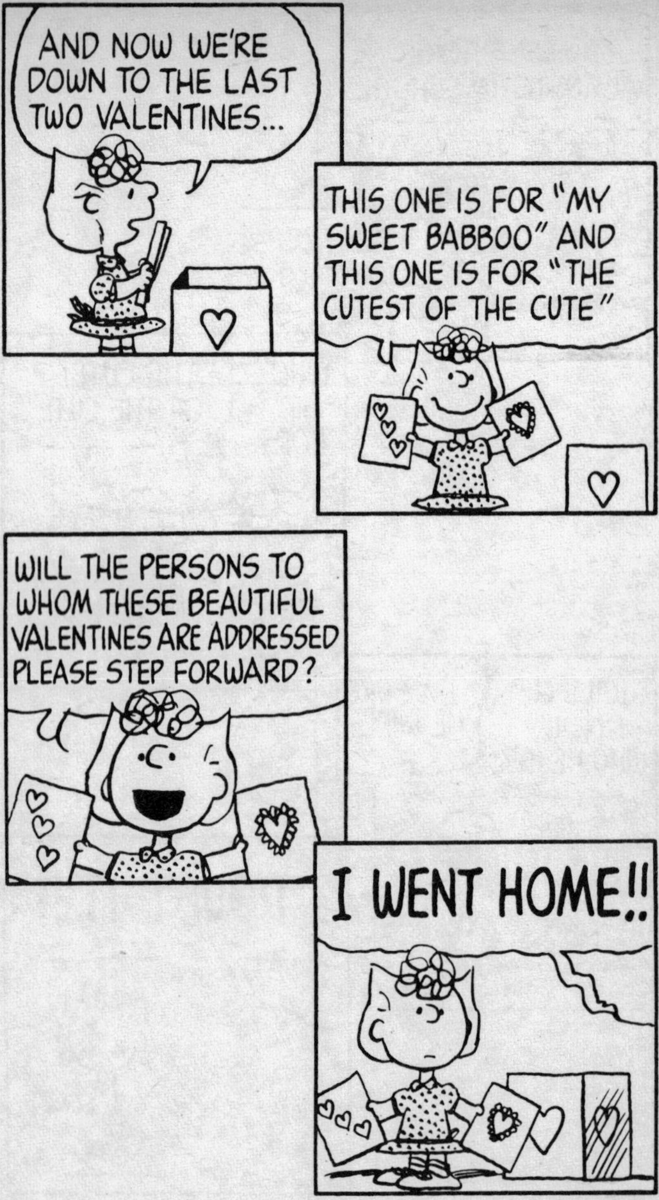
AND NOW WE'RE DOWN TO THE LAST TWO VALENTINES...
THIS ONE IS FOR "MY SWEET BABBOO" AND THIS ONE IS FOR "THE CUTEST OF THE CUTE"
WILL THE PERSONS TO WHOM THESE BEAUTIFUL VALENTINES ARE ADDRESSED PLEASE STEP FORWARD?
I WENT HOME!!

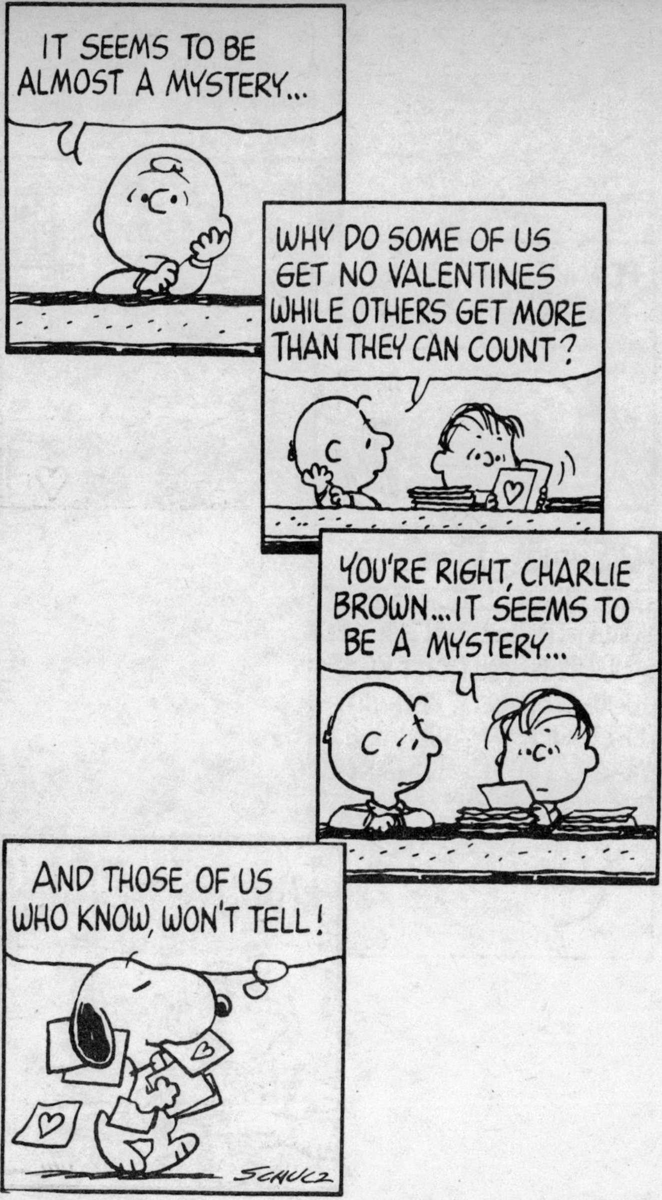
IT SEEMS TO BE ALMOST A MYSTERY...
WHY DO SOME OF US GET NO VALENTINES WHILE OTHERS GET MORE THAN THEY CAN COUNT?
YOU'RE RIGHT, CHARLIE BROWN...IT SEEMS TO BE A MYSTERY...
AND THOSE OF US WHO KNOW, WON'T TELL!
SCHULZ

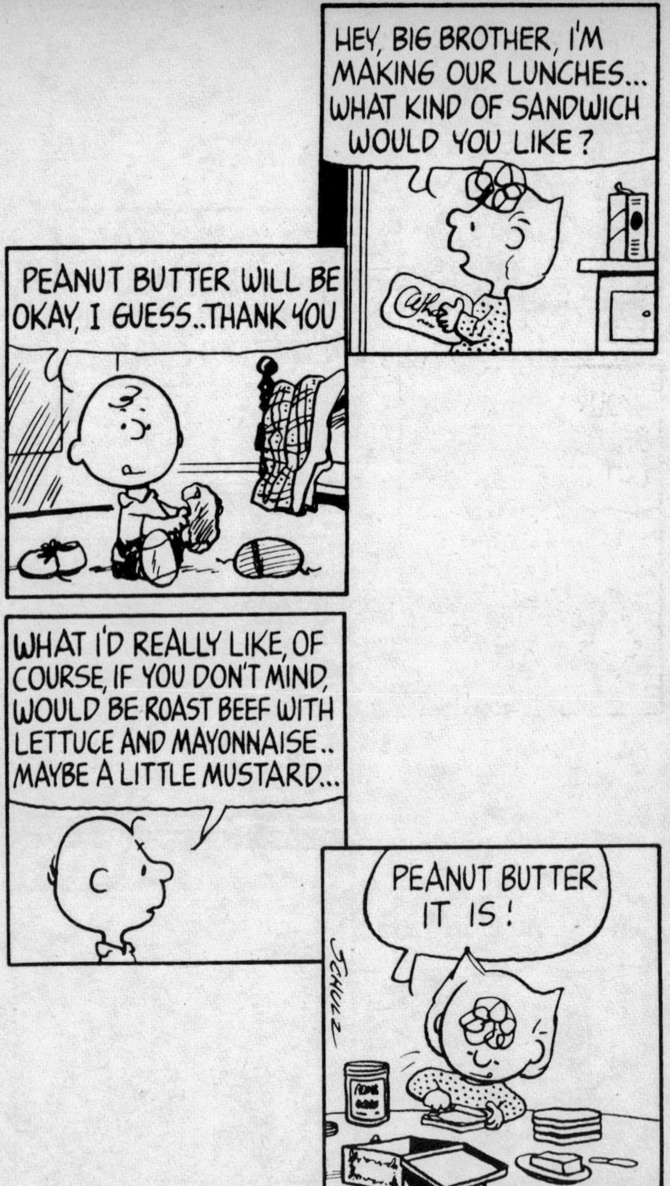
HEY, BIG BROTHER, I'M MAKING OUR LUNCHES... WHAT KIND OF SANDWICH WOULD YOU LIKE?
PEANUT BUTTER WILL BE OKAY, I GUESS..THANK YOU
WHAT I'D REALLY LIKE, OF COURSE, IF YOU DON'T MIND, WOULD BE ROAST BEEF WITH LETTUCE AND MAYONNAISE.. MAYBE A LITTLE MUSTARD...
PEANUT BUTTER IT IS!
SCHULZ

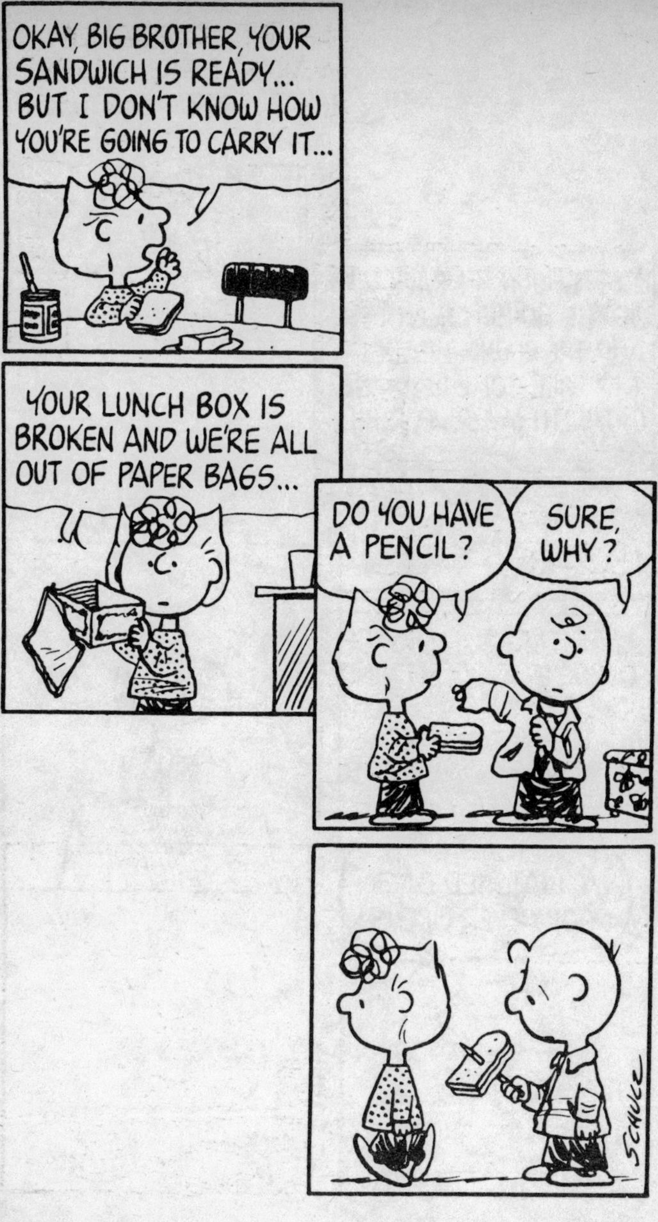
OKAY, BIG BROTHER, YOUR SANDWICH IS READY... BUT I DON'T KNOW HOW YOU'RE GOING TO CARRY IT...
YOUR LUNCH BOX IS BROKEN AND WE'RE ALL OUT OF PAPER BAGS...
DO YOU HAVE A PENCIL?
SURE, WHY?
SCHULZ

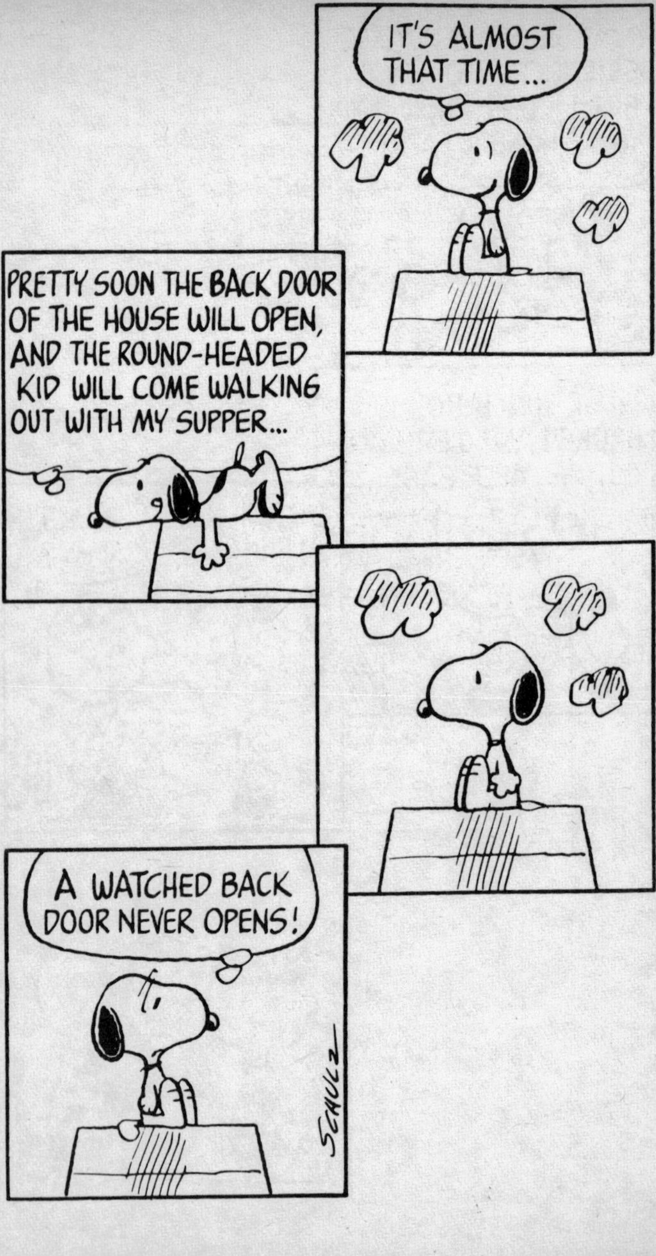
IT'S ALMOST THAT TIME...
PRETTY SOON THE BACK DOOR OF THE HOUSE WILL OPEN, AND THE ROUND-HEADED KID WILL COME WALKING OUT WITH MY SUPPER...
A WATCHED BACK DOOR NEVER OPENS!
SCHULZ

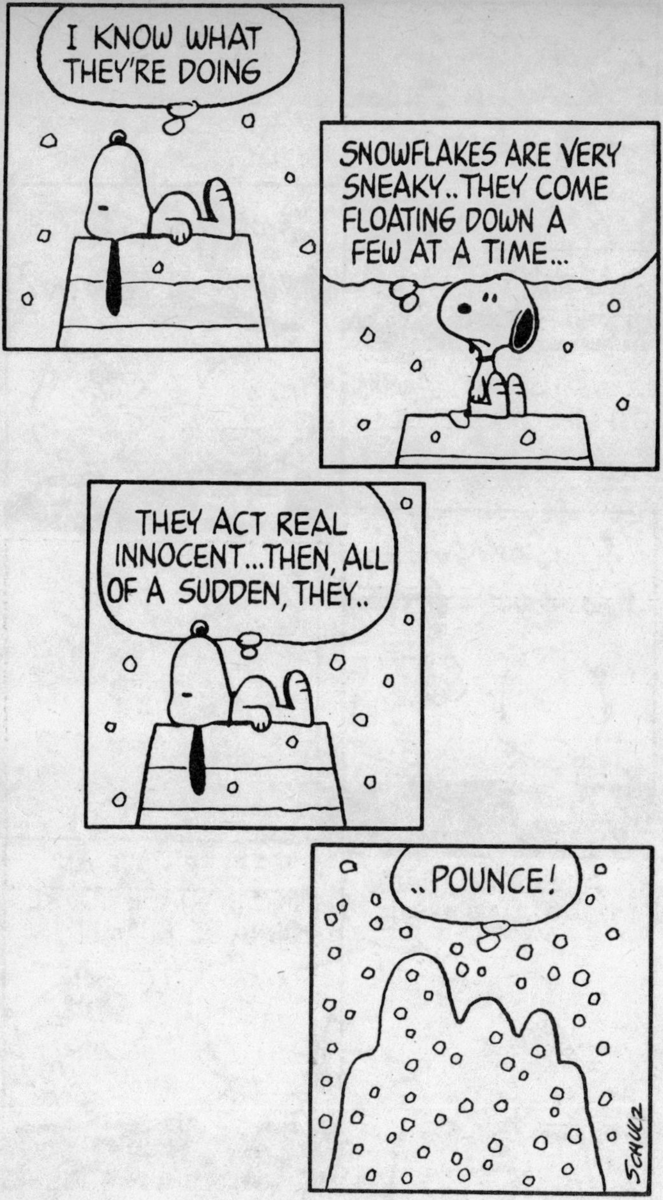
I KNOW WHAT THEY'RE DOING
SNOWFLAKES ARE VERY SNEAKY..THEY COME FLOATING DOWN A FEW AT A TIME...
THEY ACT REAL INNOCENT...THEN, ALL OF A SUDDEN, THEY..
..POUNCE!
SCHULZ

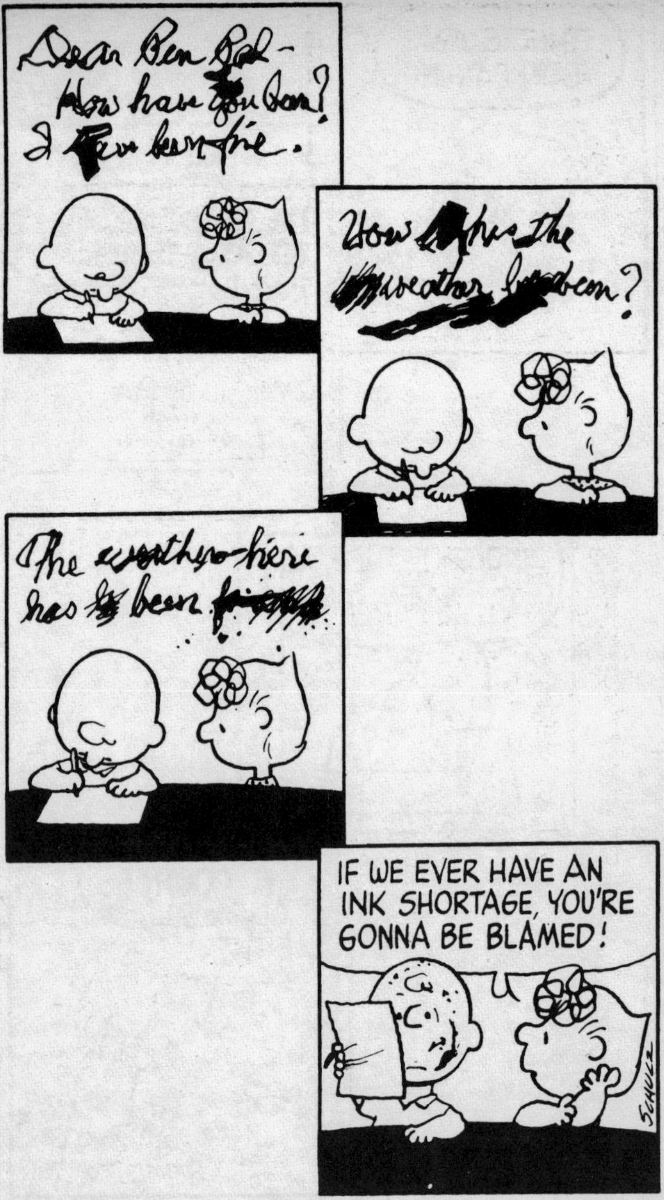

How have you been?
The weather here has been
IF WE EVER HAVE AN INK SHORTAGE, YOU'RE GONNA BE BLAMED!
SCHULZ

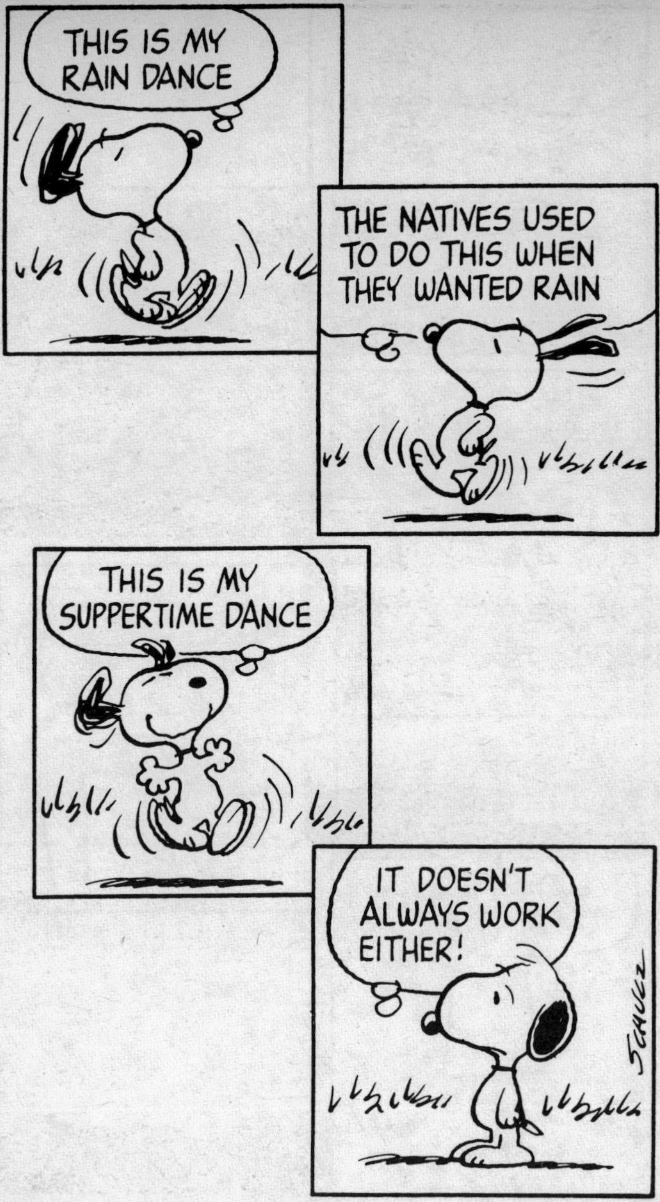
THIS IS MY RAIN DANCE
THE NATIVES USED TO DO THIS WHEN THEY WANTED RAIN
THIS IS MY SUPPERTIME DANCE
IT DOESN'T ALWAYS WORK EITHER!
SCHULZ

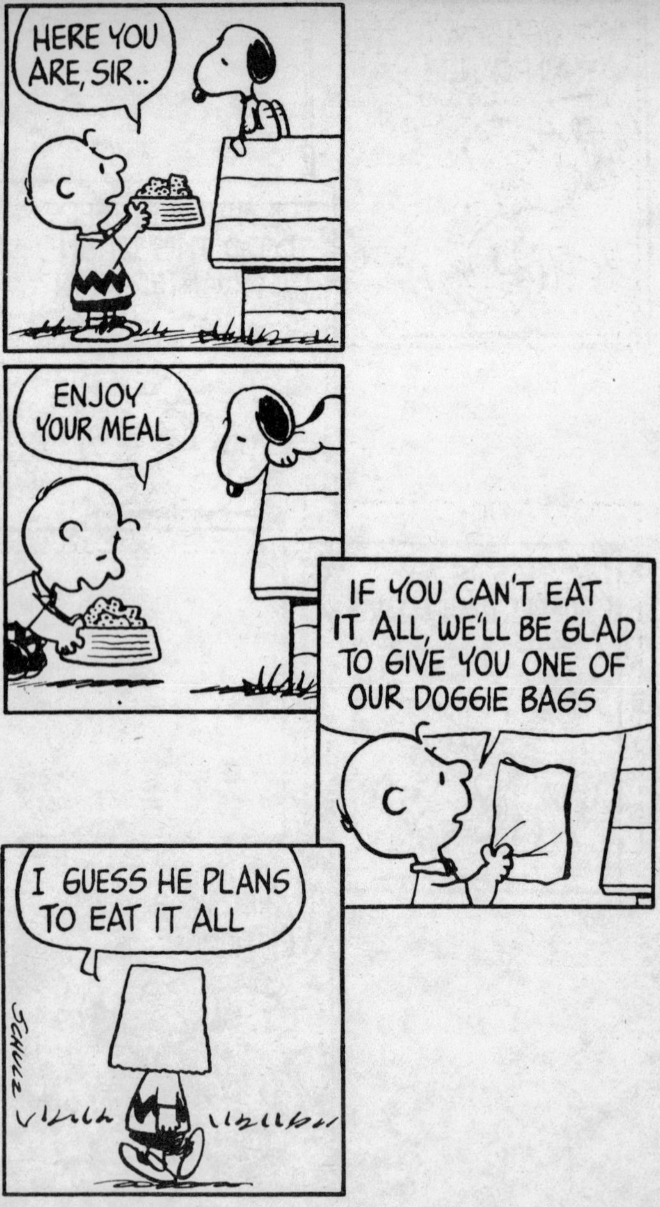
HERE YOU ARE, SIR..
ENJOY YOUR MEAL
IF YOU CAN'T EAT IT ALL, WE'LL BE GLAD TO GIVE YOU ONE OF OUR DOGGIE BAGS
I GUESS HE PLANS TO EAT IT ALL
SCHULZ

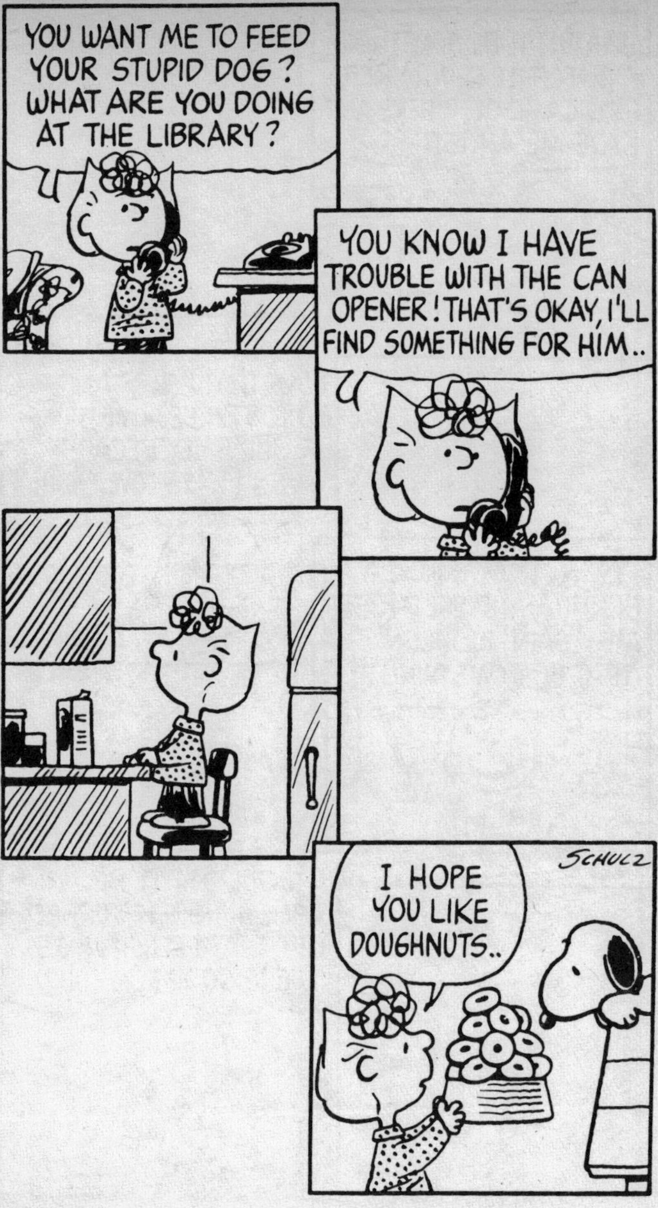
YOU WANT ME TO FEED YOUR STUPID DOG? WHAT ARE YOU DOING AT THE LIBRARY?
YOU KNOW I HAVE TROUBLE WITH THE CAN OPENER! THAT'S OKAY, I'LL FIND SOMETHING FOR HIM..
I HOPE YOU LIKE DOUGHNUTS..
SCHULZ

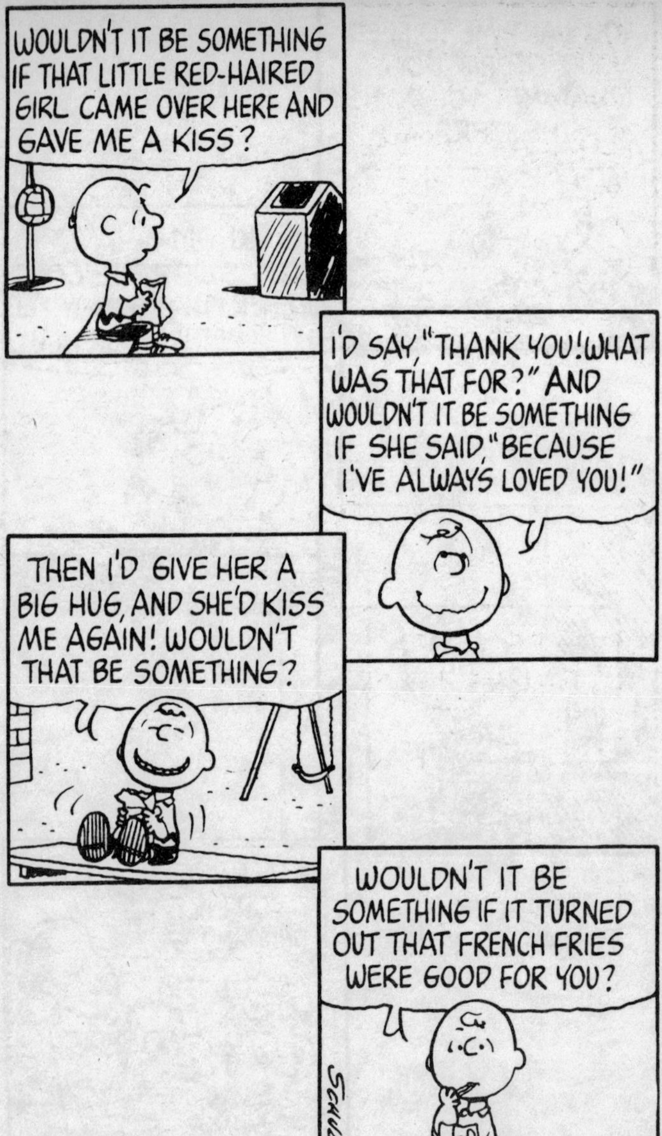
WOULDN'T IT BE SOMETHING IF THAT LITTLE RED-HAIRED GIRL CAME OVER HERE AND GAVE ME A KISS?
I'D SAY, "THANK YOU! WHAT WAS THAT FOR?" AND WOULDN'T IT BE SOMETHING IF SHE SAID, "BECAUSE I'VE ALWAYS LOVED YOU!"
THEN I'D GIVE HER A BIG HUG, AND SHE'D KISS ME AGAIN! WOULDN'T THAT BE SOMETHING?
WOULDN'T IT BE SOMETHING IF IT TURNED OUT THAT FRENCH FRIES WERE GOOD FOR YOU?
SCHULZ

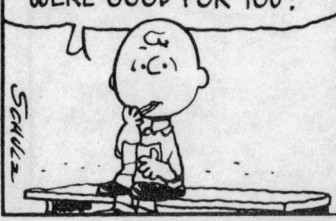

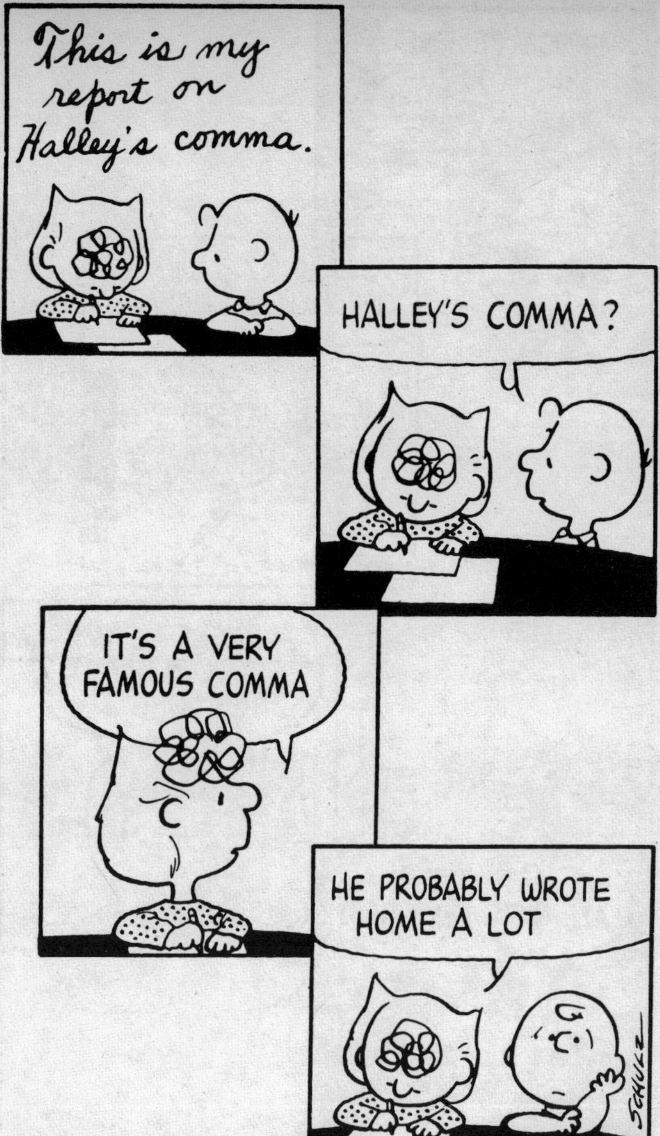
This is my report on Halley's comma.
HALLEY'S COMMA?
IT'S A VERY FAMOUS COMMA
HE PROBABLY WROTE HOME A LOT
SCHULZ

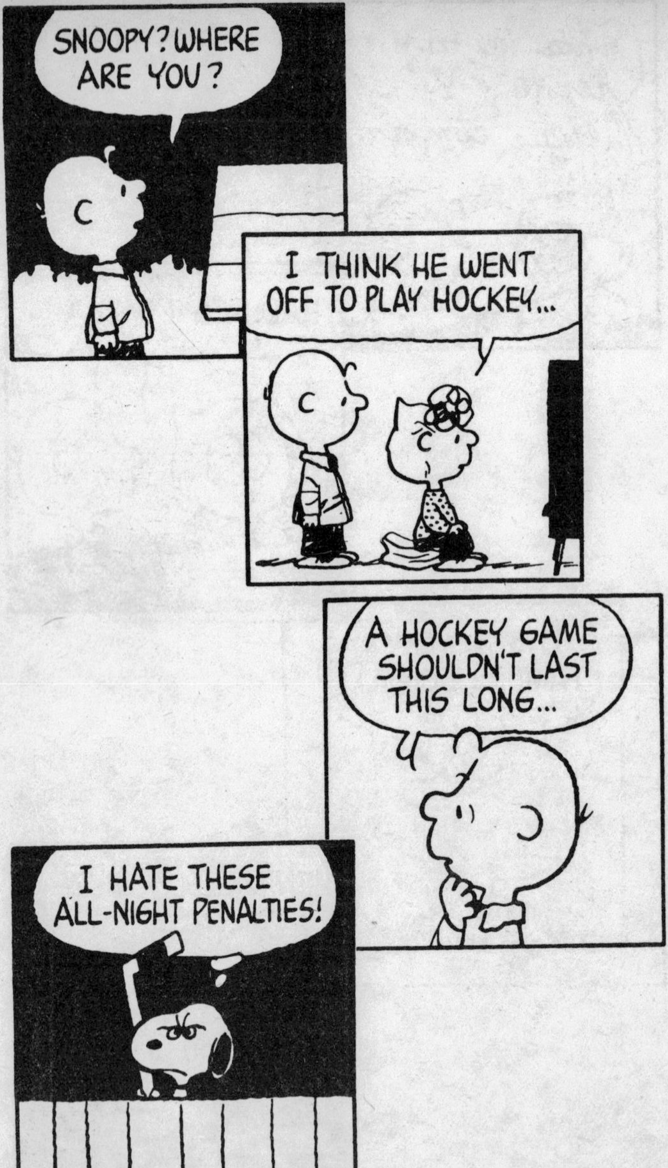
SNOOPY? WHERE ARE YOU?
I THINK HE WENT OFF TO PLAY HOCKEY...
A HOCKEY GAME SHOULDN'T LAST THIS LONG...
I HATE THESE ALL-NIGHT PENALTIES!
SCHULZ

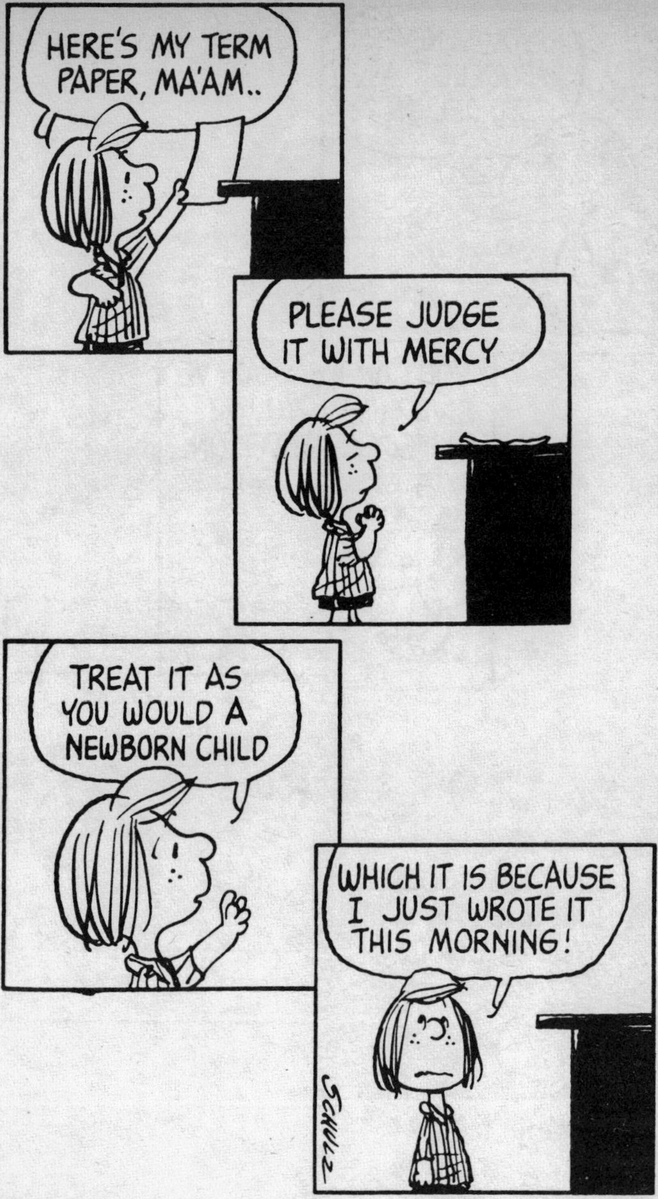
HERE'S MY TERM PAPER, MA'AM..
PLEASE JUDGE IT WITH MERCY
TREAT IT AS YOU WOULD A NEWBORN CHILD
WHICH IT IS BECAUSE I JUST WROTE IT THIS MORNING!
SCHULZ

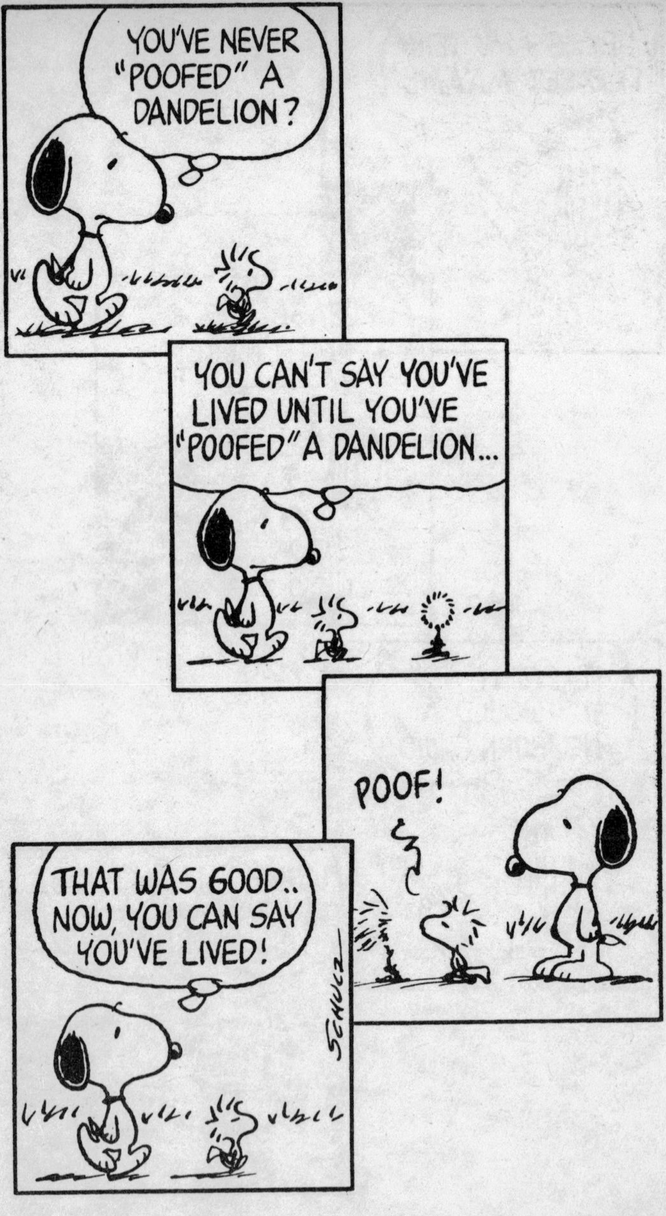
YOU'VE NEVER "POOFED" A DANDELION?
YOU CAN'T SAY YOU'VE LIVED UNTIL YOU'VE "POOFED" A DANDELION...
POOF!
THAT WAS GOOD.. NOW, YOU CAN SAY YOU'VE LIVED!
SCHULZ

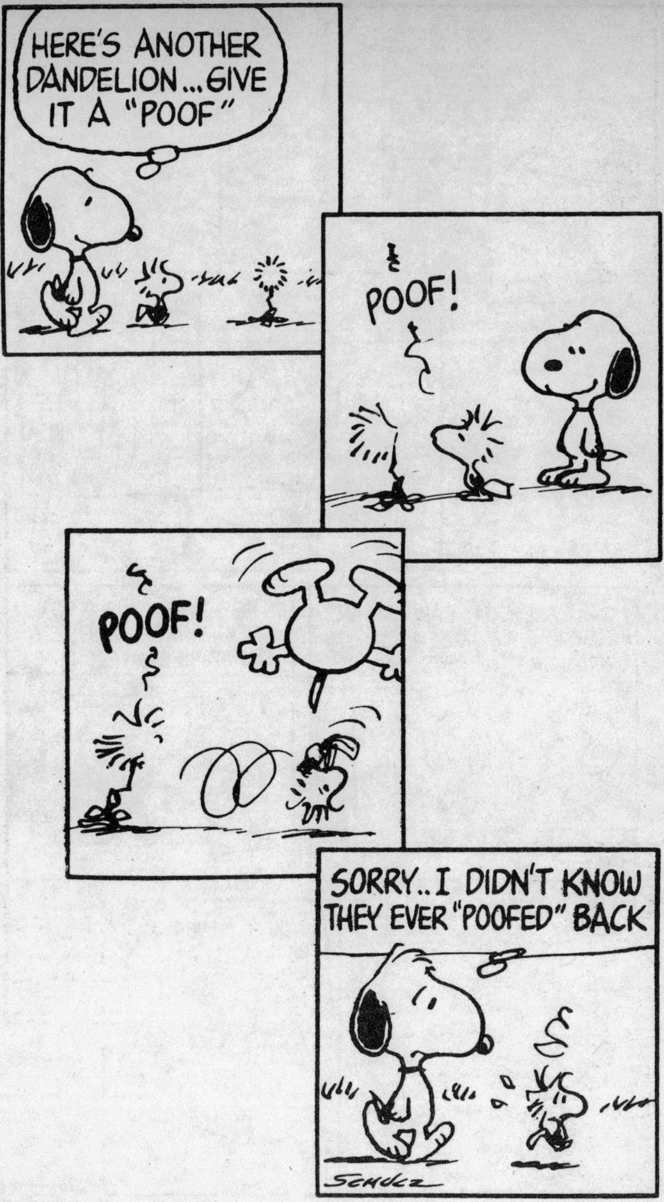
HERE'S ANOTHER DANDELION...GIVE IT A "POOF"
POOF!
POOF!
SORRY..I DIDN'T KNOW THEY EVER "POOFED" BACK
SCHULZ

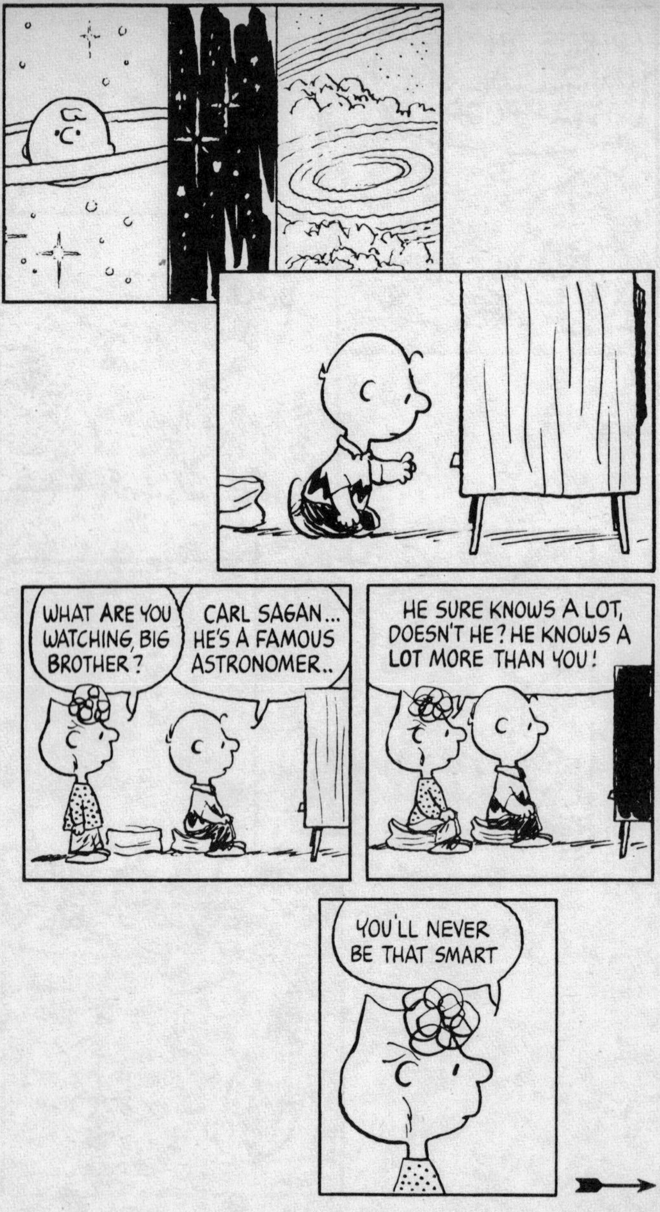
WHAT ARE YOU WATCHING, BIG BROTHER?
CARL SAGAN... HE'S A FAMOUS ASTRONOMER..
HE SURE KNOWS A LOT, DOESN'T HE? HE KNOWS A LOT MORE THAN YOU!
YOU'LL NEVER BE THAT SMART

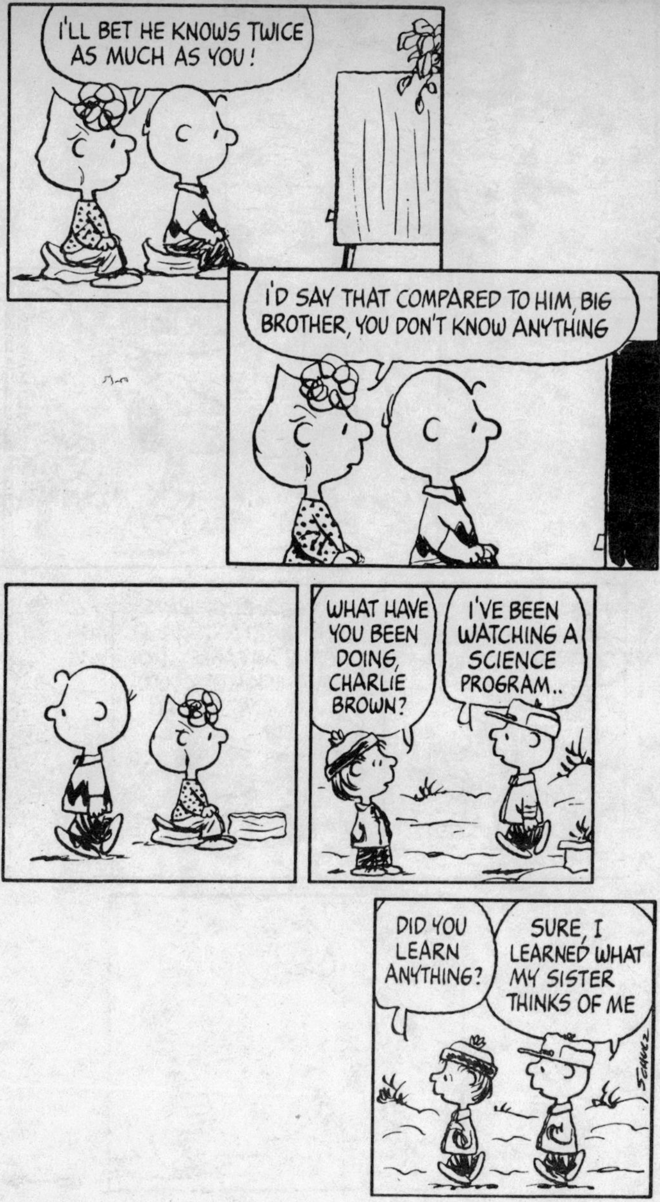
I'LL BET HE KNOWS TWICE AS MUCH AS YOU!
I'D SAY THAT COMPARED TO HIM, BIG BROTHER, YOU DON'T KNOW ANYTHING
WHAT HAVE YOU BEEN DOING, CHARLIE BROWN?
I'VE BEEN WATCHING A SCIENCE PROGRAM..
DID YOU LEARN ANYTHING?
SURE, I LEARNED WHAT MY SISTER THINKS OF ME
SCHULZ

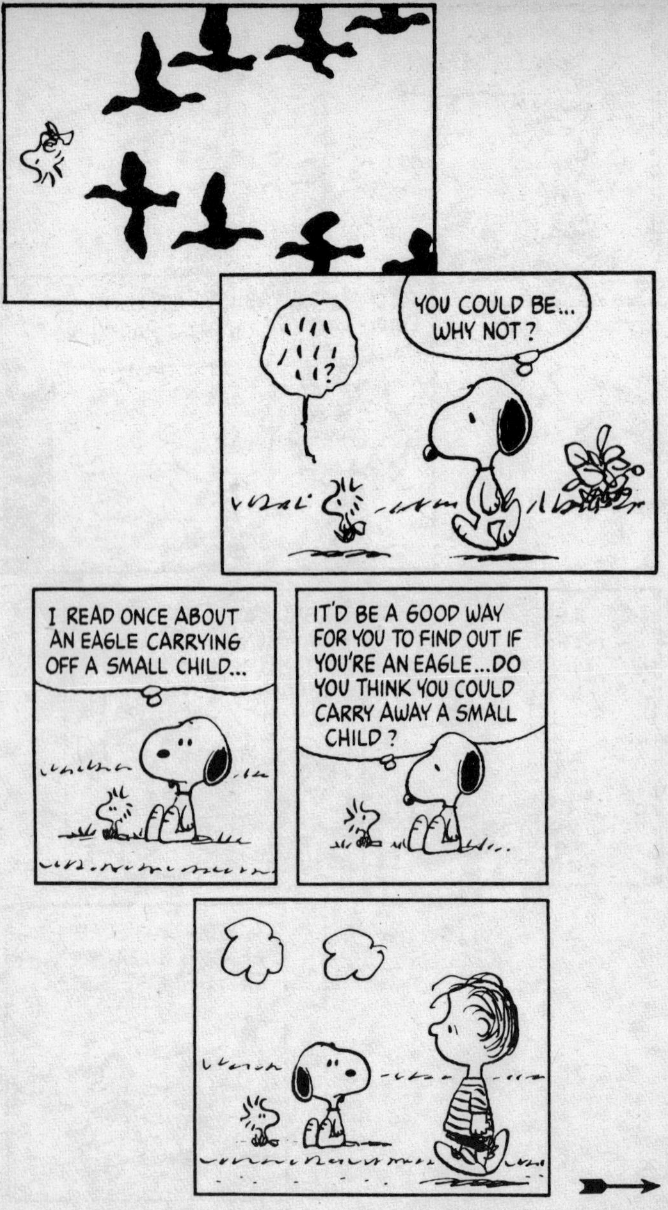
YOU COULD BE... WHY NOT?
I READ ONCE ABOUT AN EAGLE CARRYING OFF A SMALL CHILD...
IT'D BE A GOOD WAY FOR YOU TO FIND OUT IF YOU'RE AN EAGLE...DO YOU THINK YOU COULD CARRY AWAY A SMALL CHILD?

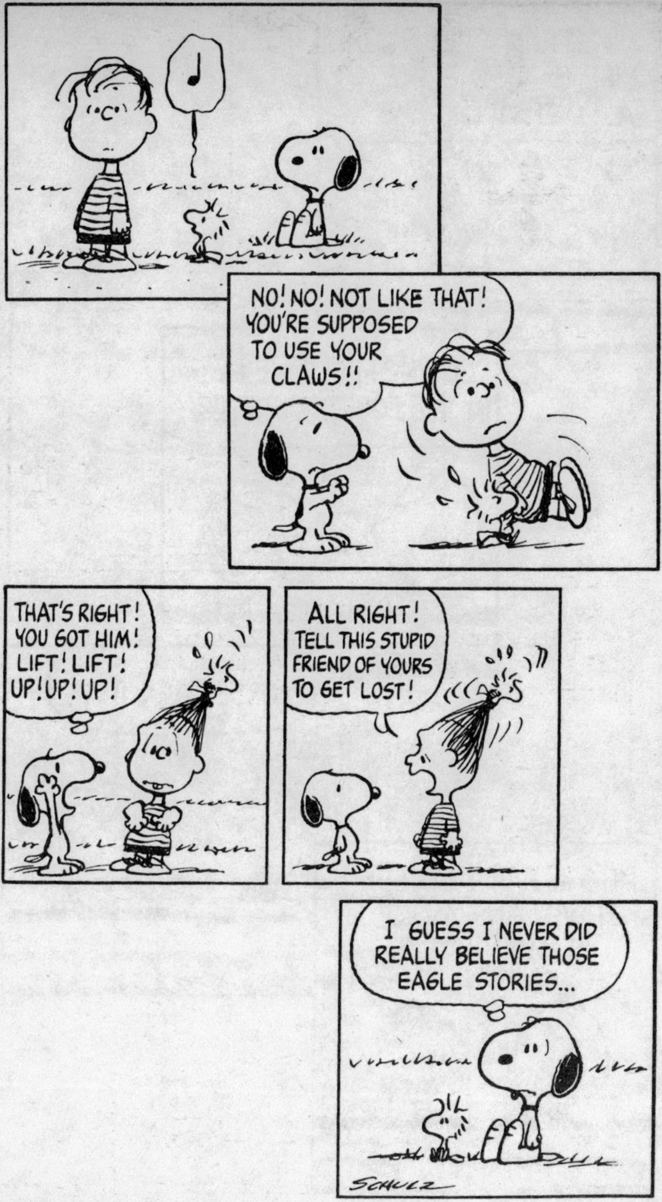
NO! NO! NOT LIKE THAT! YOU'RE SUPPOSED TO USE YOUR CLAWS!!
THAT'S RIGHT! YOU GOT HIM! LIFT! LIFT! UP! UP! UP!
ALL RIGHT! TELL THIS STUPID FRIEND OF YOURS TO GET LOST!
I GUESS I NEVER DID REALLY BELIEVE THOSE EAGLE STORIES...
SCHULZ

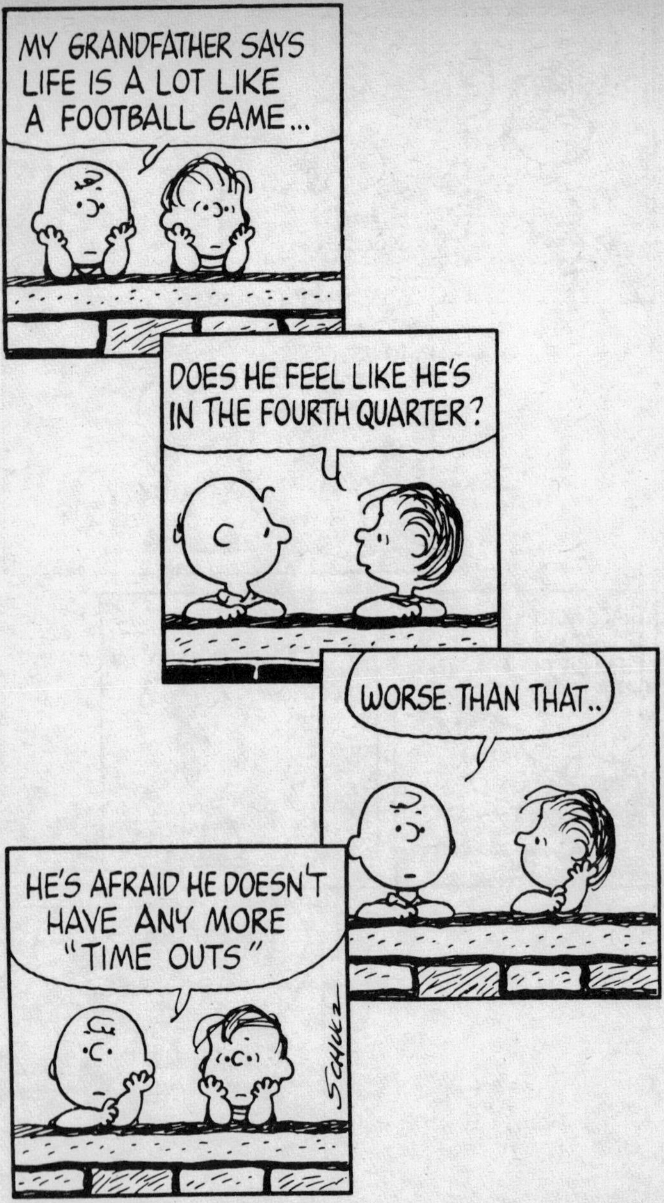
MY GRANDFATHER SAYS LIFE IS A LOT LIKE A FOOTBALL GAME...
DOES HE FEEL LIKE HE'S IN THE FOURTH QUARTER?
WORSE THAN THAT..
HE'S AFRAID HE DOESN'T HAVE ANY MORE "TIME OUTS"
SCHULZ

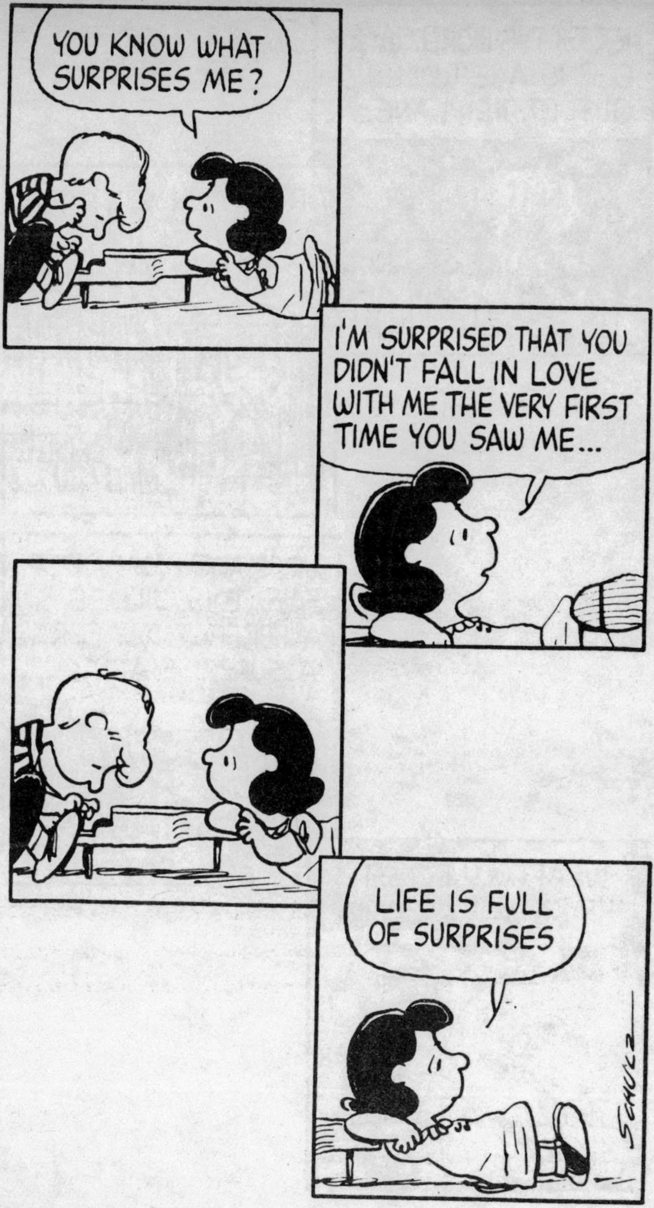
YOU KNOW WHAT SURPRISES ME?
I'M SURPRISED THAT YOU DIDN'T FALL IN LOVE WITH ME THE VERY FIRST TIME YOU SAW ME...
LIFE IS FULL OF SURPRISES
SCHULZ

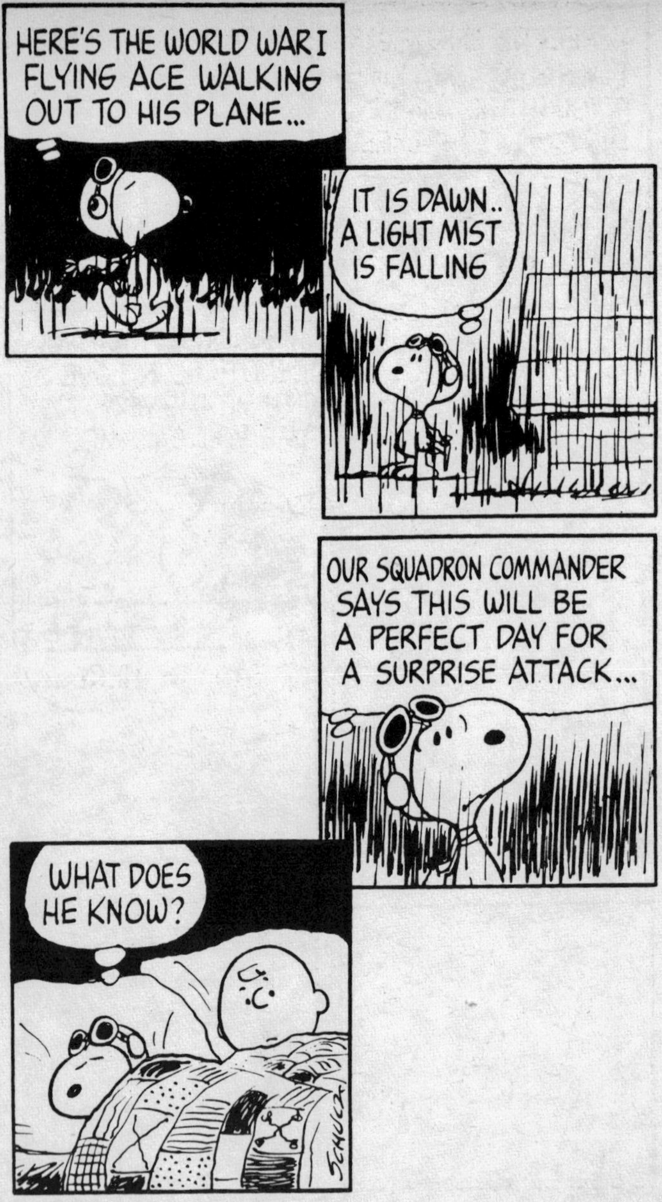
HERE'S THE WORLD WAR I FLYING ACE WALKING OUT TO HIS PLANE...
IT IS DAWN.. A LIGHT MIST IS FALLING
OUR SQUADRON COMMANDER SAYS THIS WILL BE A PERFECT DAY FOR A SURPRISE ATTACK...
WHAT DOES HE KNOW?
SCHULZ

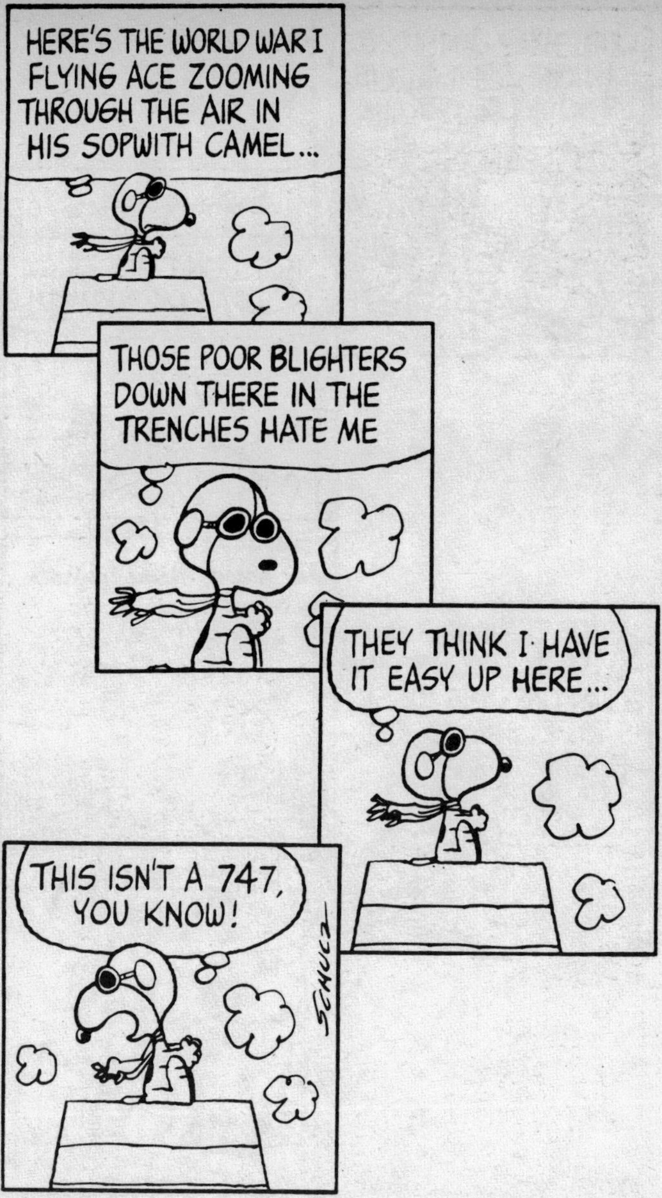
HERE'S THE WORLD WAR I FLYING ACE ZOOMING THROUGH THE AIR IN HIS SOPWITH CAMEL...
THOSE POOR BLIGHTERS DOWN THERE IN THE TRENCHES HATE ME
THEY THINK I HAVE IT EASY UP HERE...
THIS ISN'T A 747, YOU KNOW!
SCHULZ

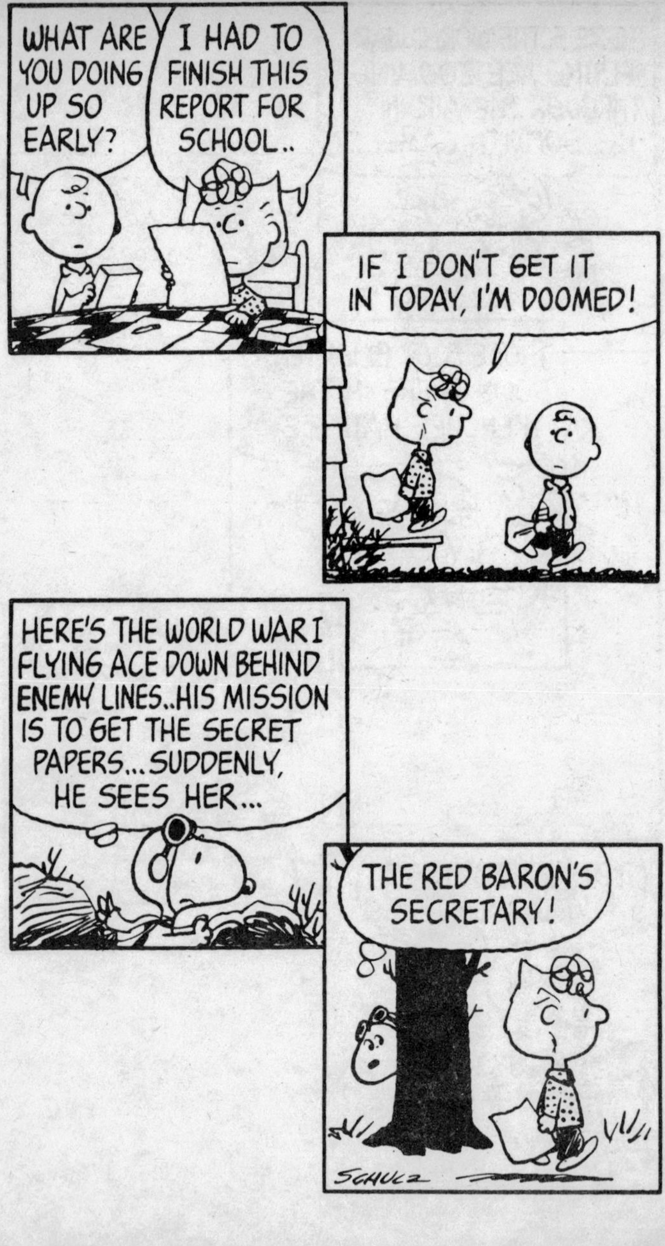
WHAT ARE YOU DOING UP SO EARLY?
I HAD TO FINISH THIS REPORT FOR SCHOOL..
IF I DON'T GET IT IN TODAY, I'M DOOMED!
HERE'S THE WORLD WAR I FLYING ACE DOWN BEHIND ENEMY LINES..HIS MISSION IS TO GET THE SECRET PAPERS...SUDDENLY, HE SEES HER...
THE RED BARON'S SECRETARY!
SCHULZ

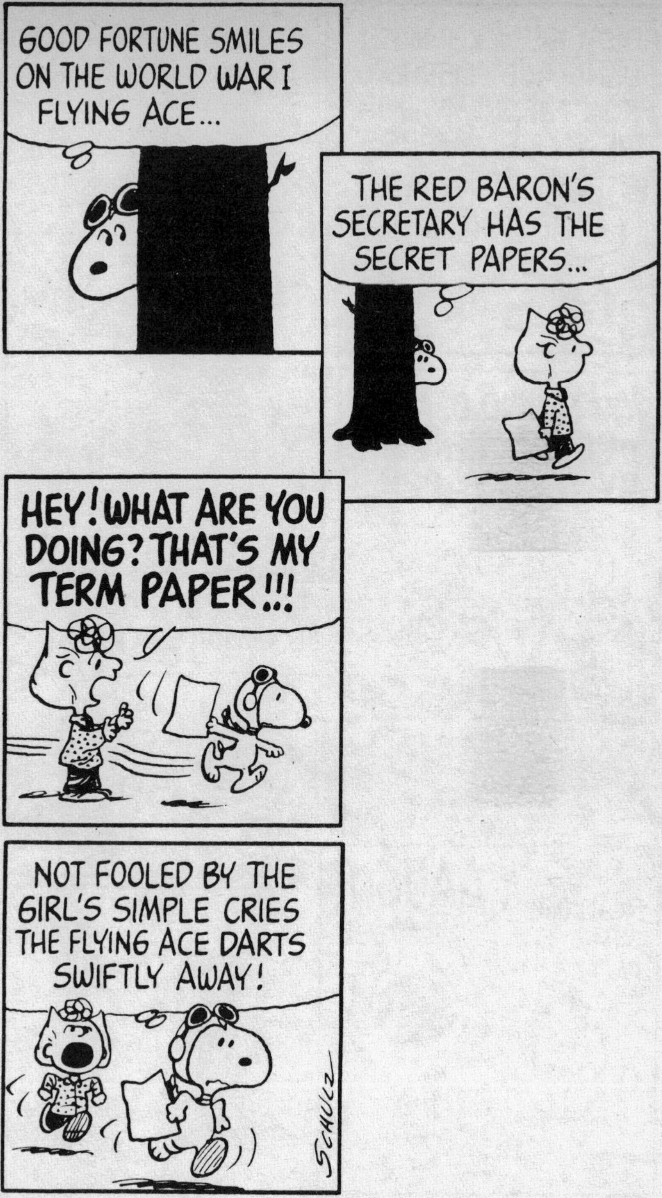
GOOD FORTUNE SMILES ON THE WORLD WAR I FLYING ACE...
THE RED BARON'S SECRETARY HAS THE SECRET PAPERS...
HEY! WHAT ARE YOU DOING? THAT'S MY TERM PAPER!!!
NOT FOOLED BY THE GIRL'S SIMPLE CRIES THE FLYING ACE DARTS SWIFTLY AWAY!
SCHULZ

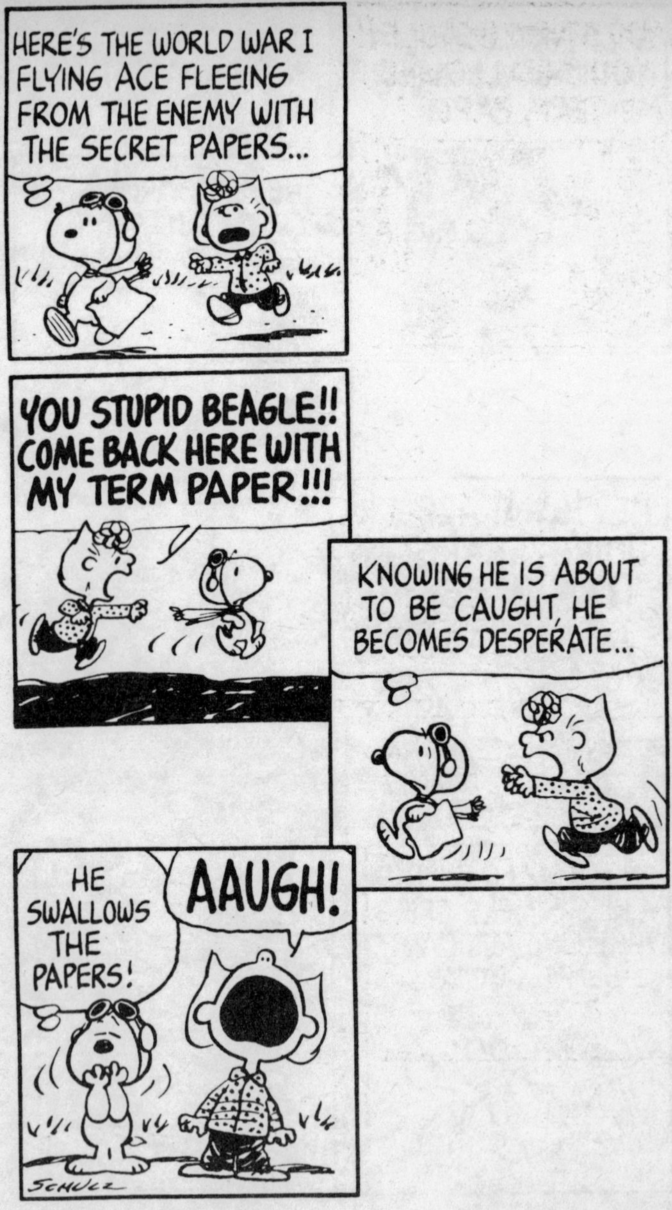
HERE'S THE WORLD WAR I FLYING ACE FLEEING FROM THE ENEMY WITH THE SECRET PAPERS...
YOU STUPID BEAGLE!! COME BACK HERE WITH MY TERM PAPER!!!
KNOWING HE IS ABOUT TO BE CAUGHT, HE BECOMES DESPERATE...
HE SWALLOWS THE PAPERS!
AAUGH!
SCHULZ

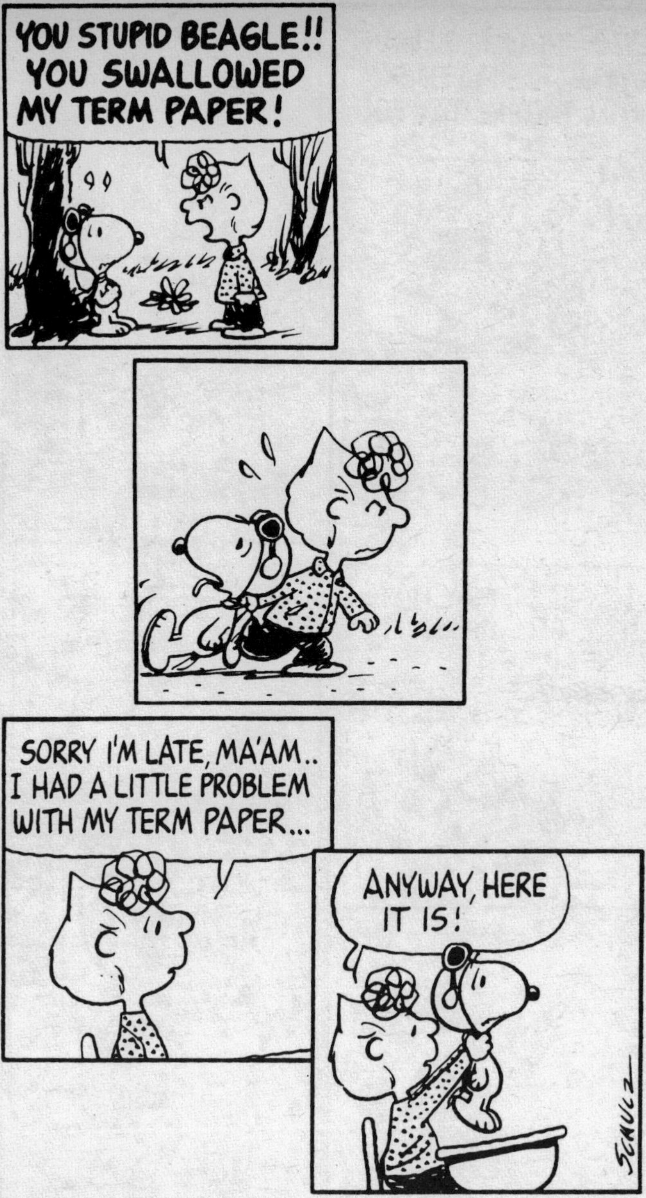
YOU STUPID BEAGLE!! YOU SWALLOWED MY TERM PAPER!
SORRY I'M LATE, MA'AM.. I HAD A LITTLE PROBLEM WITH MY TERM PAPER...
ANYWAY, HERE IT IS!
SCHULZ

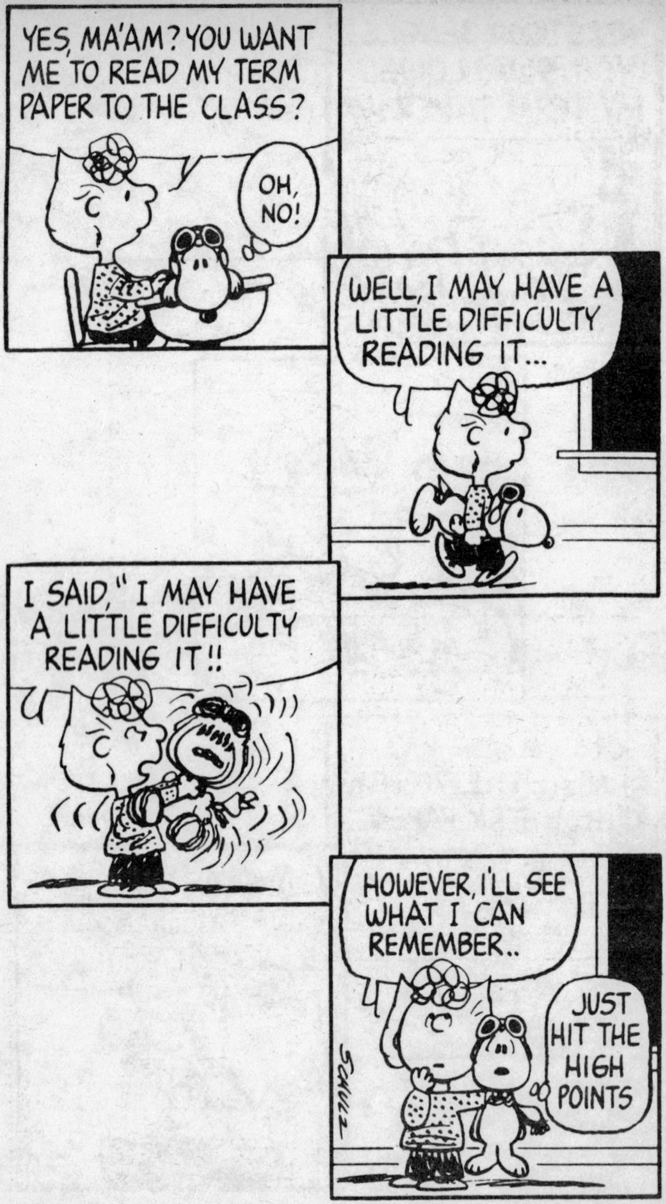

YES, MA'AM? YOU WANT ME TO READ MY TERM PAPER TO THE CLASS?
OH, NO!
WELL, I MAY HAVE A LITTLE DIFFICULTY READING IT...
I SAID, "I MAY HAVE A LITTLE DIFFICULTY READING IT!!
HOWEVER, I'LL SEE WHAT I CAN REMEMBER..
JUST HIT THE HIGH POINTS
SCHULZ

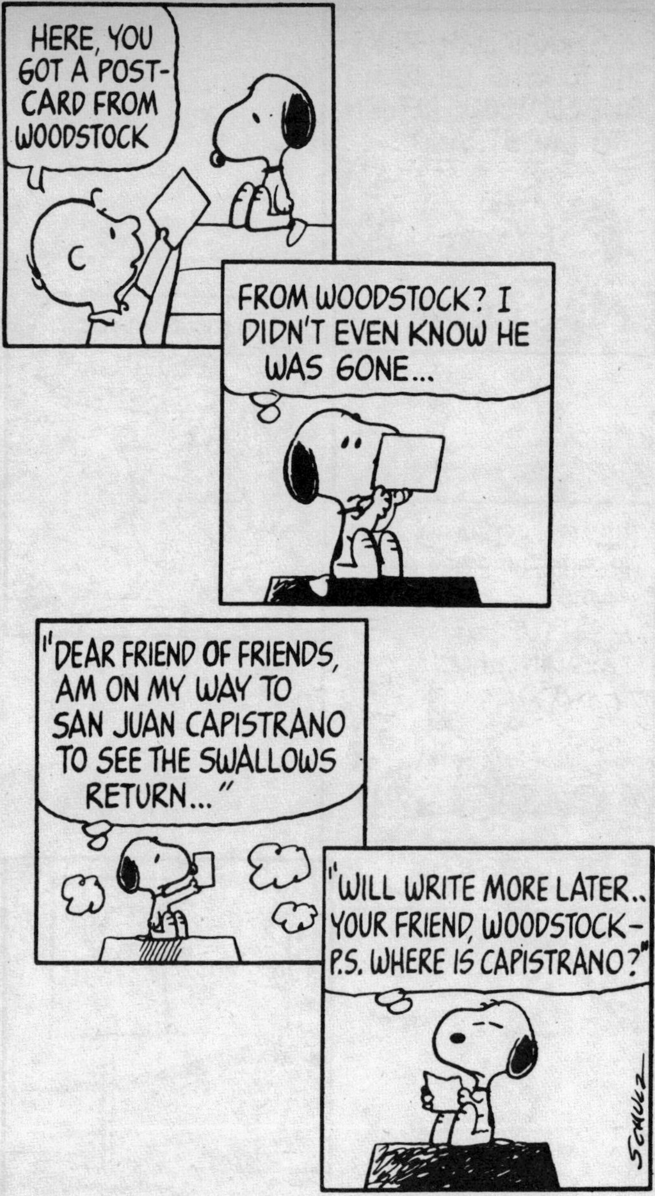
HERE, YOU GOT A POST-CARD FROM WOODSTOCK
FROM WOODSTOCK? I DIDN'T EVEN KNOW HE WAS GONE...
"DEAR FRIEND OF FRIENDS, AM ON MY WAY TO SAN JUAN CAPISTRANO TO SEE THE SWALLOWS RETURN..."
"WILL WRITE MORE LATER.. YOUR FRIEND, WOODSTOCK- P.S. WHERE IS CAPISTRANO?"
SCHULZ

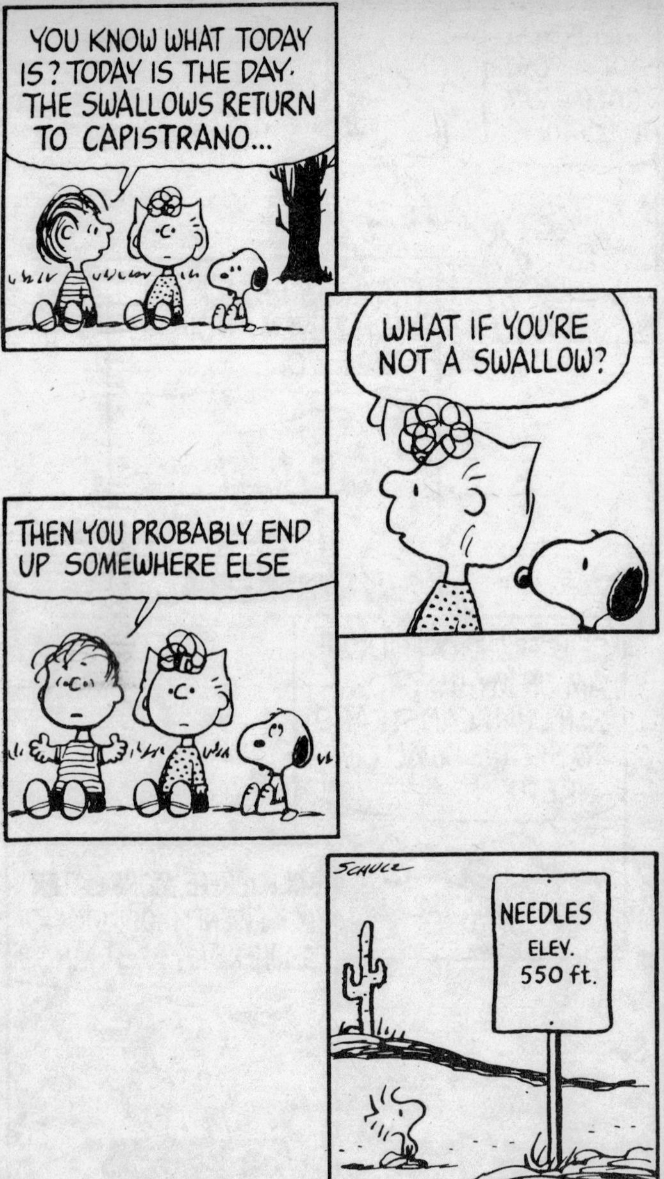
YOU KNOW WHAT TODAY IS? TODAY IS THE DAY THE SWALLOWS RETURN TO CAPISTRANO...
WHAT IF YOU'RE NOT A SWALLOW?
THEN YOU PROBABLY END UP SOMEWHERE ELSE
SCHULZ
NEEDLES
ELEV.
550 ft.

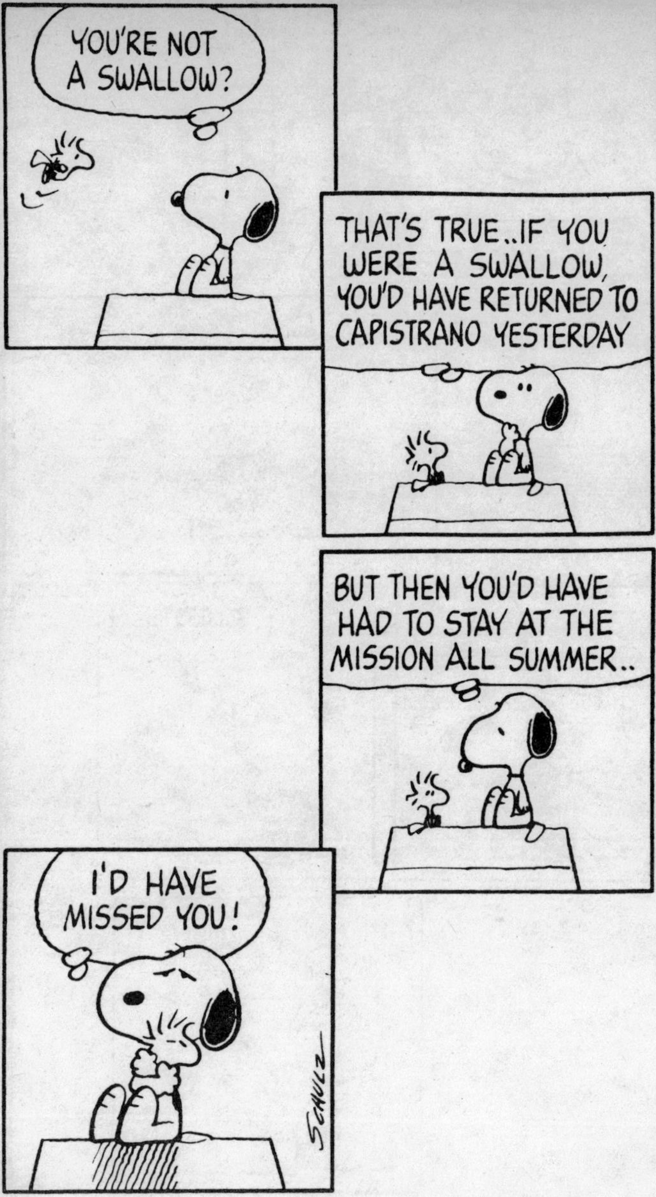
YOU'RE NOT A SWALLOW?
THAT'S TRUE..IF YOU WERE A SWALLOW, YOU'D HAVE RETURNED TO CAPISTRANO YESTERDAY
BUT THEN YOU'D HAVE HAD TO STAY AT THE MISSION ALL SUMMER..
I'D HAVE MISSED YOU!
SCHULZ

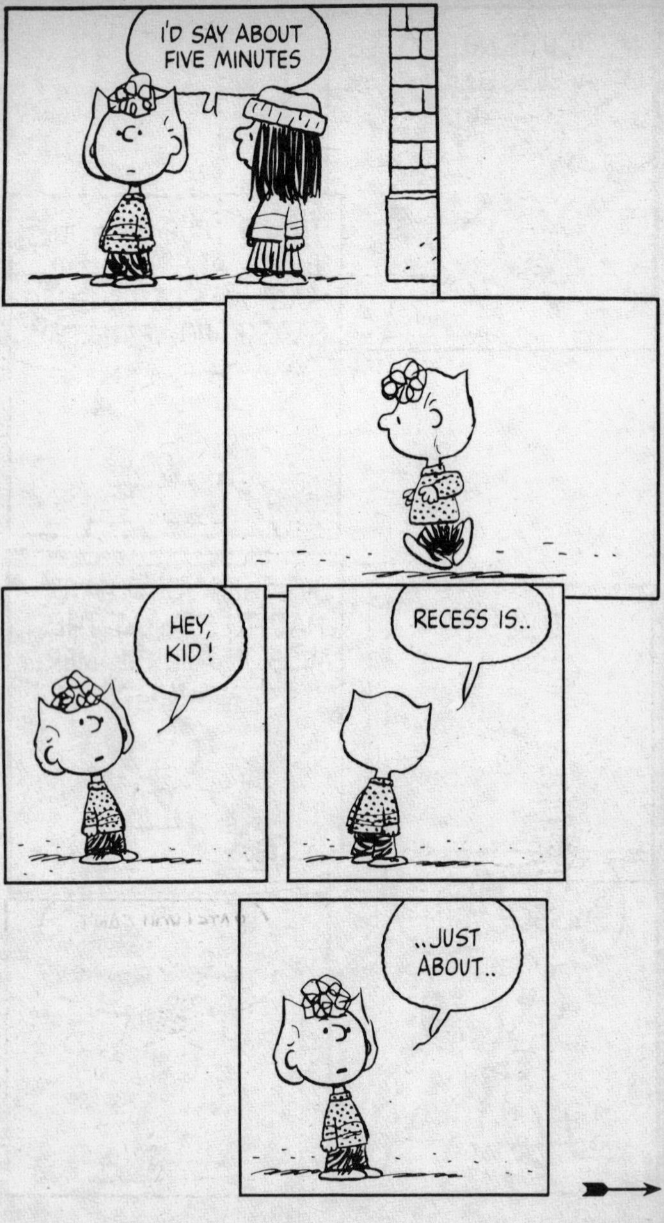
I'D SAY ABOUT FIVE MINUTES
HEY, KID!
RECESS IS..
..JUST ABOUT..

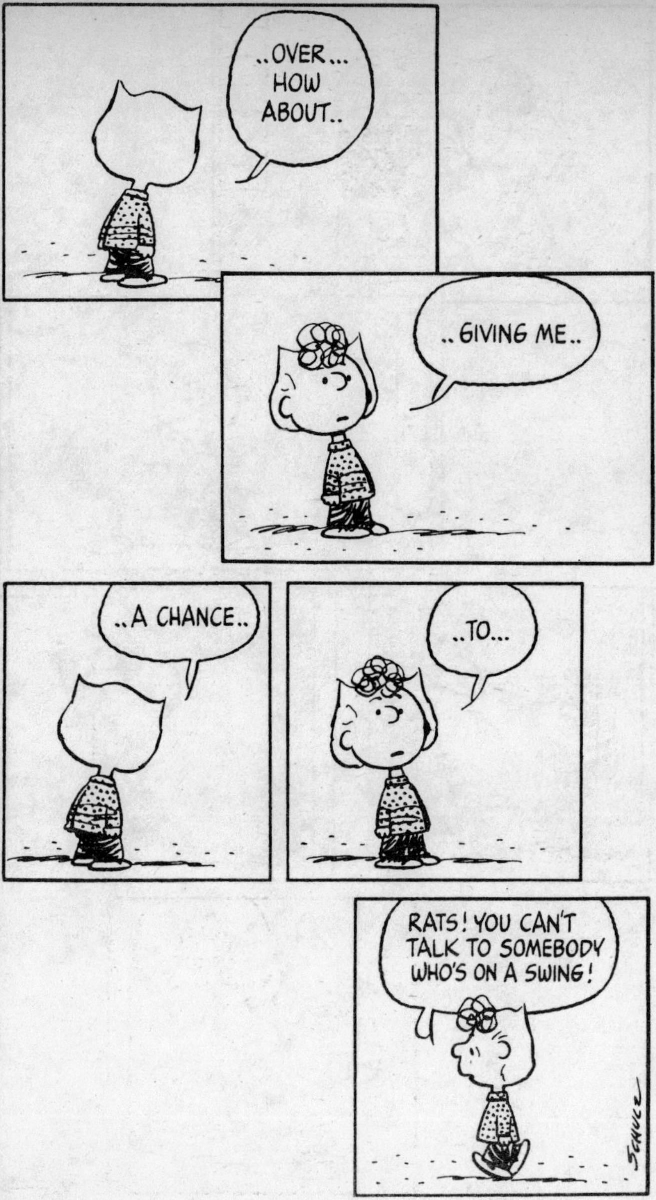
..OVER... HOW ABOUT..
..GIVING ME..
..A CHANCE..
..TO...
RATS! YOU CAN'T TALK TO SOMEBODY WHO'S ON A SWING!
SCHULZ

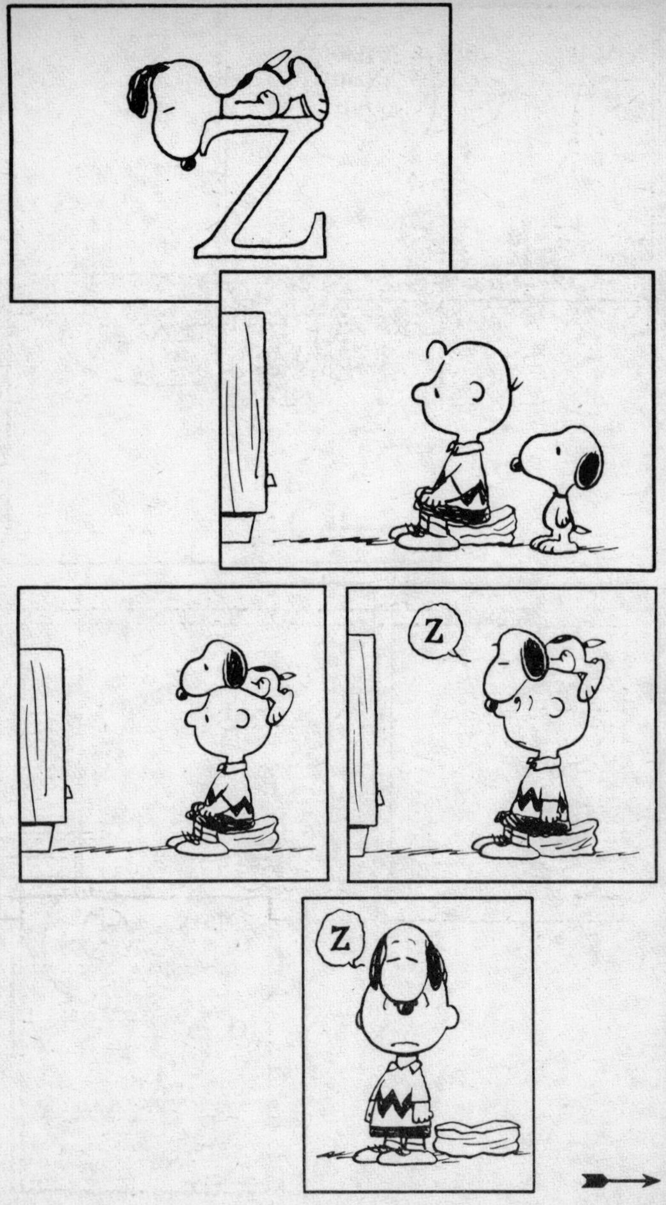
Z
Z
Z

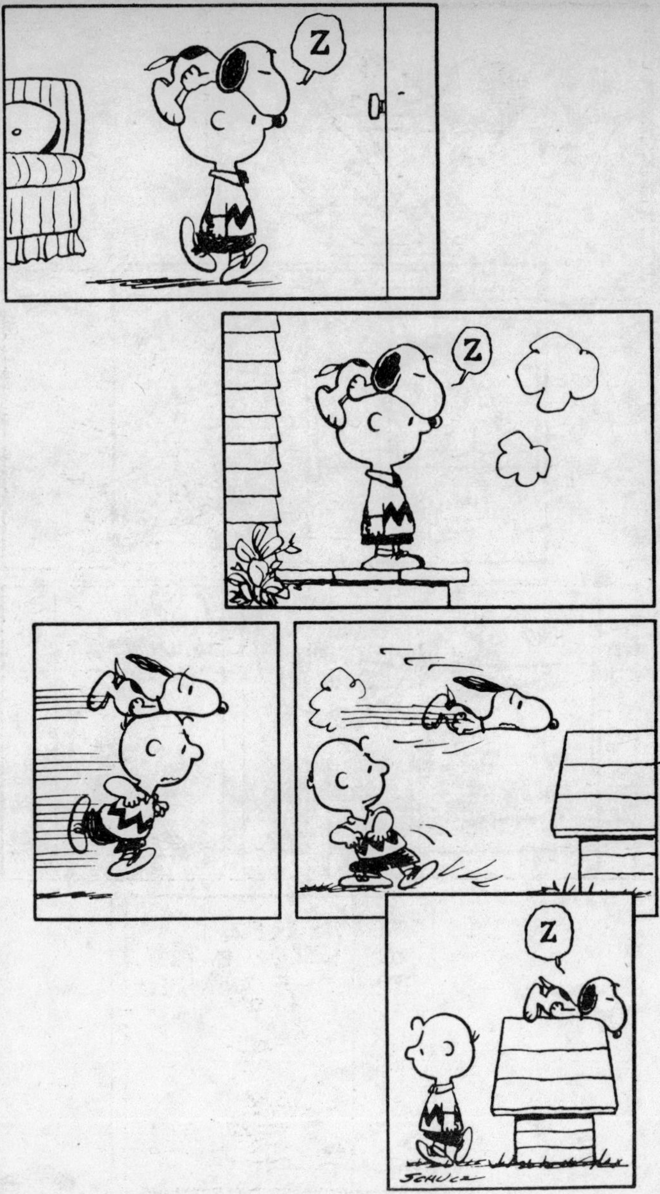
Z
Z
Z
SCHULZ

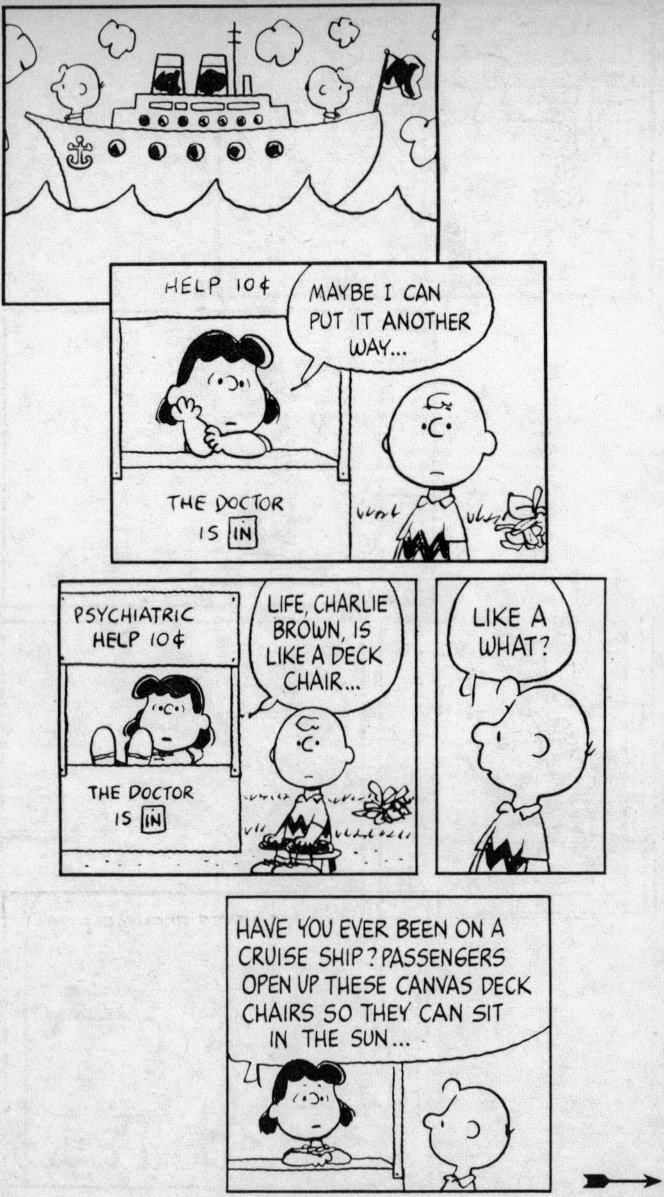
HELP 10¢
MAYBE I CAN PUT IT ANOTHER WAY...
THE DOCTOR IS IN
PSYCHIATRIC HELP 10¢
LIFE, CHARLIE BROWN, IS LIKE A DECK CHAIR...
THE DOCTOR IS IN
LIKE A WHAT?
HAVE YOU EVER BEEN ON A CRUISE SHIP? PASSENGERS OPEN UP THESE CANVAS DECK CHAIRS SO THEY CAN SIT IN THE SUN...

SOME PEOPLE PLACE THEIR CHAIRS FACING THE REAR OF THE SHIP SO THEY CAN SEE WHERE THEY'VE BEEN...

THE DOCTOR IS IN

OTHER PEOPLE FACE THEIR CHAIRS FORWARD...THEY WANT TO SEE WHERE THEY'RE GOING!

THE DOCTOR IS IN

PSYCHIATRIC HELP 10¢

ON THE CRUISE SHIP OF LIFE, CHARLIE BROWN, WHICH WAY IS YOUR DECK CHAIR FACING?

THE DOCTOR IS IN

PSYCHIATRIC HELP

I'VE NEVER BEEN ABLE TO GET ONE UNFOLDED...

THE DOCTOR IS IN

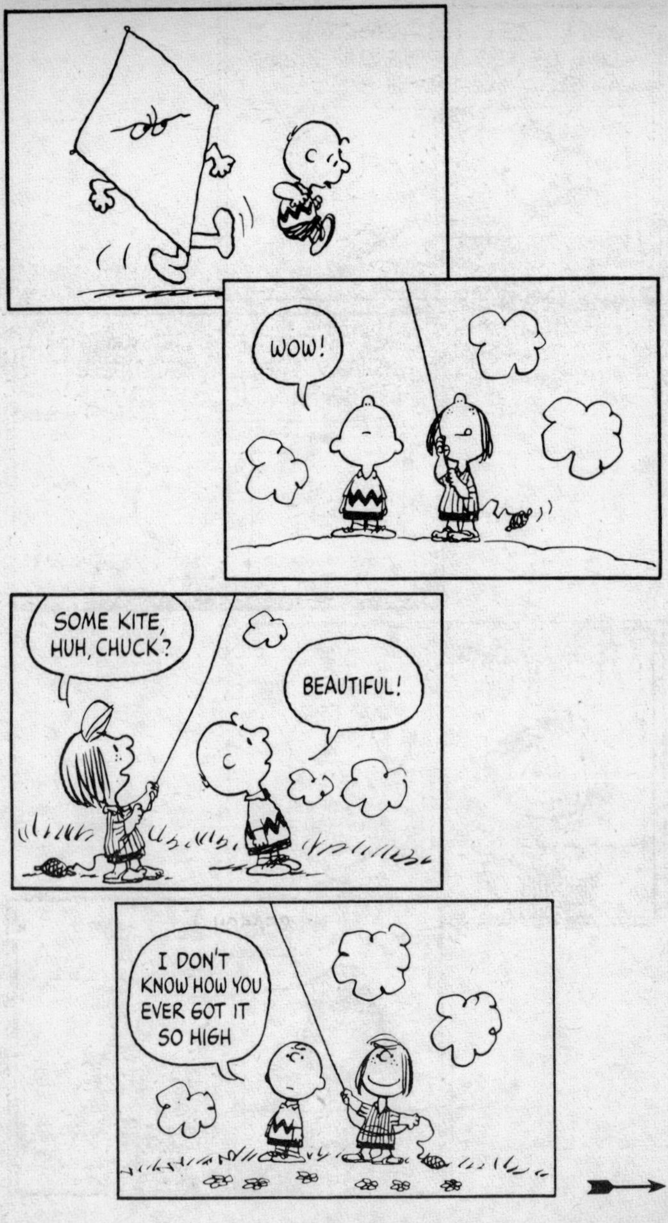
WOW!
SOME KITE, HUH, CHUCK?
BEAUTIFUL!
I DON'T KNOW HOW YOU EVER GOT IT SO HIGH

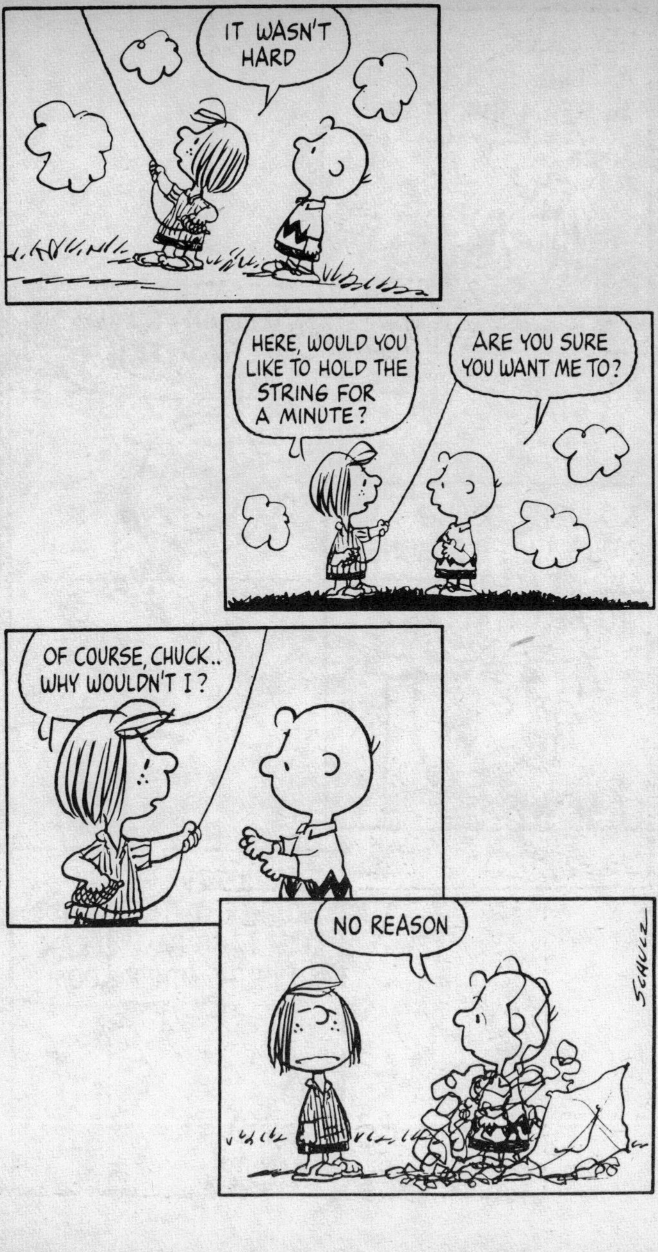
IT WASN'T HARD
HERE, WOULD YOU LIKE TO HOLD THE STRING FOR A MINUTE?
ARE YOU SURE YOU WANT ME TO?
OF COURSE, CHUCK.. WHY WOULDN'T I?
NO REASON
SCHULZ

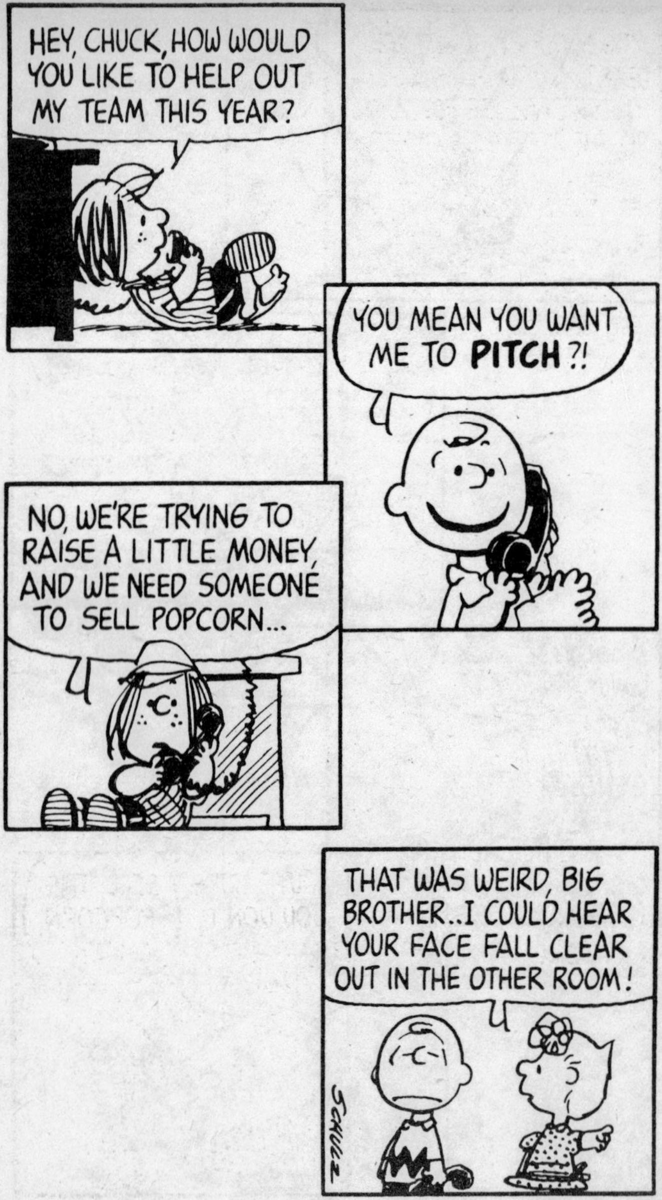

HEY, CHUCK, HOW WOULD YOU LIKE TO HELP OUT MY TEAM THIS YEAR?
YOU MEAN YOU WANT ME TO **PITCH**?!
NO, WE'RE TRYING TO RAISE A LITTLE MONEY, AND WE NEED SOMEONE TO SELL POPCORN...
THAT WAS WEIRD, BIG BROTHER..I COULD HEAR YOUR FACE FALL CLEAR OUT IN THE OTHER ROOM!
SCHULZ

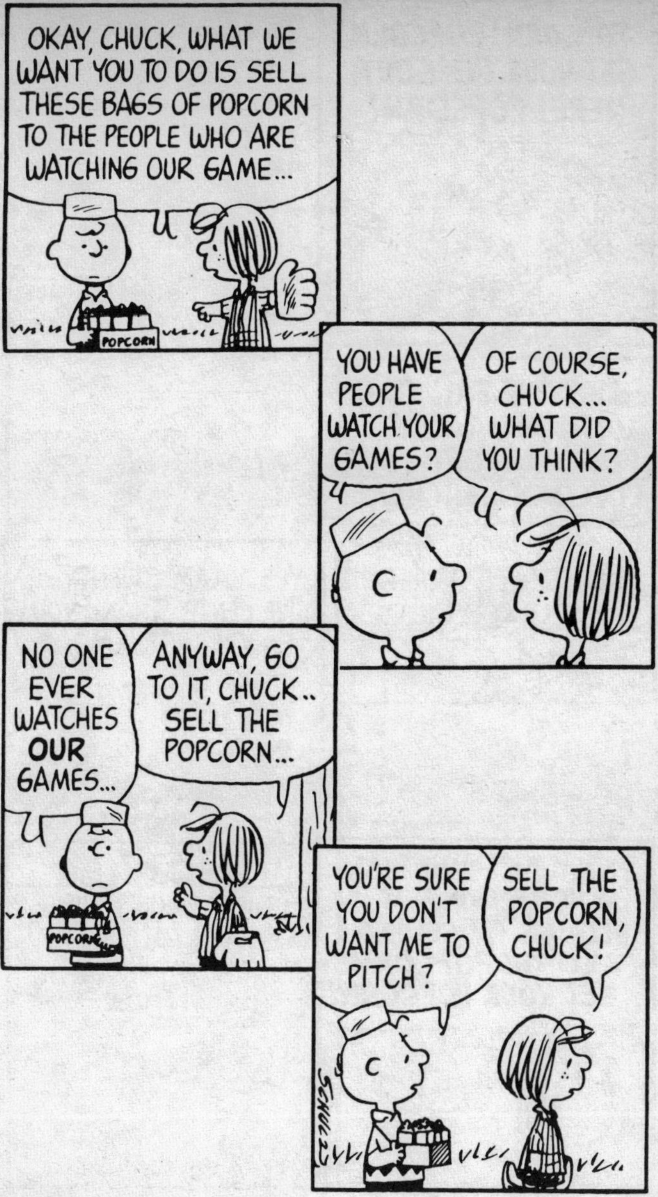
OKAY, CHUCK, WHAT WE WANT YOU TO DO IS SELL THESE BAGS OF POPCORN TO THE PEOPLE WHO ARE WATCHING OUR GAME...
POPCORN
YOU HAVE PEOPLE WATCH YOUR GAMES?
OF COURSE, CHUCK... WHAT DID YOU THINK?
NO ONE EVER WATCHES **OUR** GAMES...
ANYWAY, GO TO IT, CHUCK.. SELL THE POPCORN...
POPCORN
YOU'RE SURE YOU DON'T WANT ME TO PITCH?
SELL THE POPCORN, CHUCK!
SCHULZ

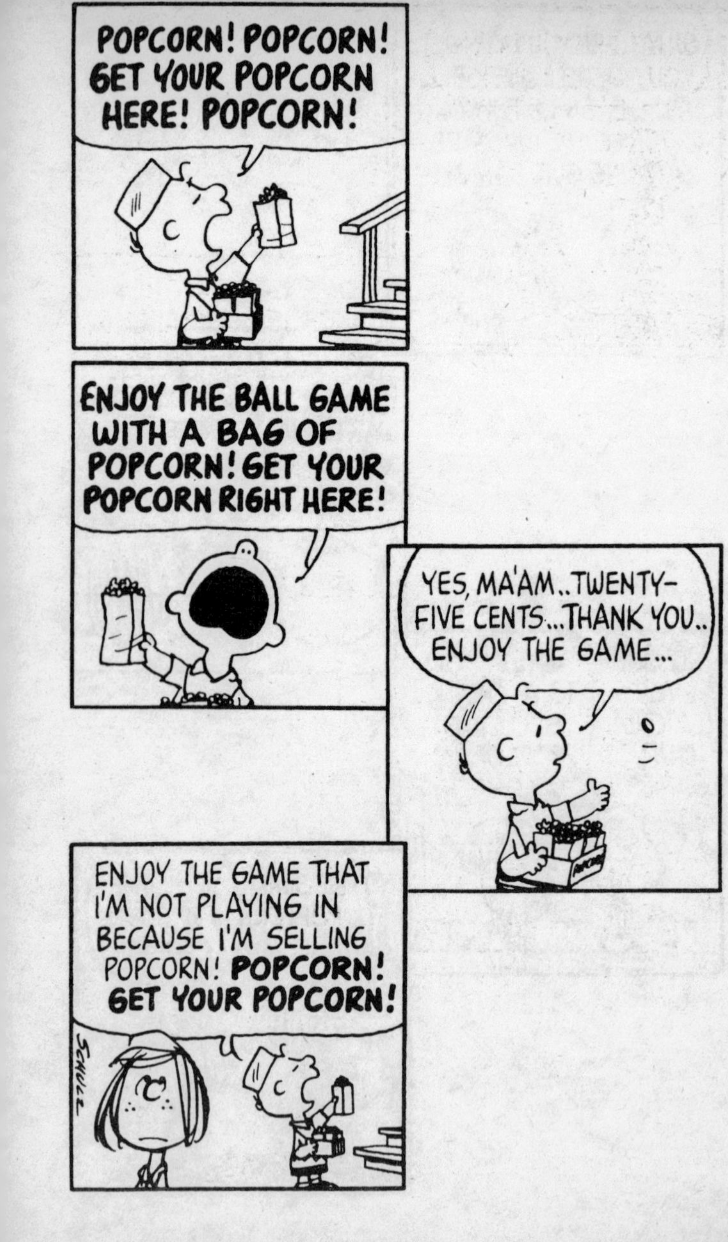
POPCORN! POPCORN! GET YOUR POPCORN HERE! POPCORN!
ENJOY THE BALL GAME WITH A BAG OF POPCORN! GET YOUR POPCORN RIGHT HERE!
YES, MA'AM.. TWENTY-FIVE CENTS... THANK YOU.. ENJOY THE GAME...
ENJOY THE GAME THAT I'M NOT PLAYING IN BECAUSE I'M SELLING POPCORN! POPCORN! GET YOUR POPCORN!
SCHULZ

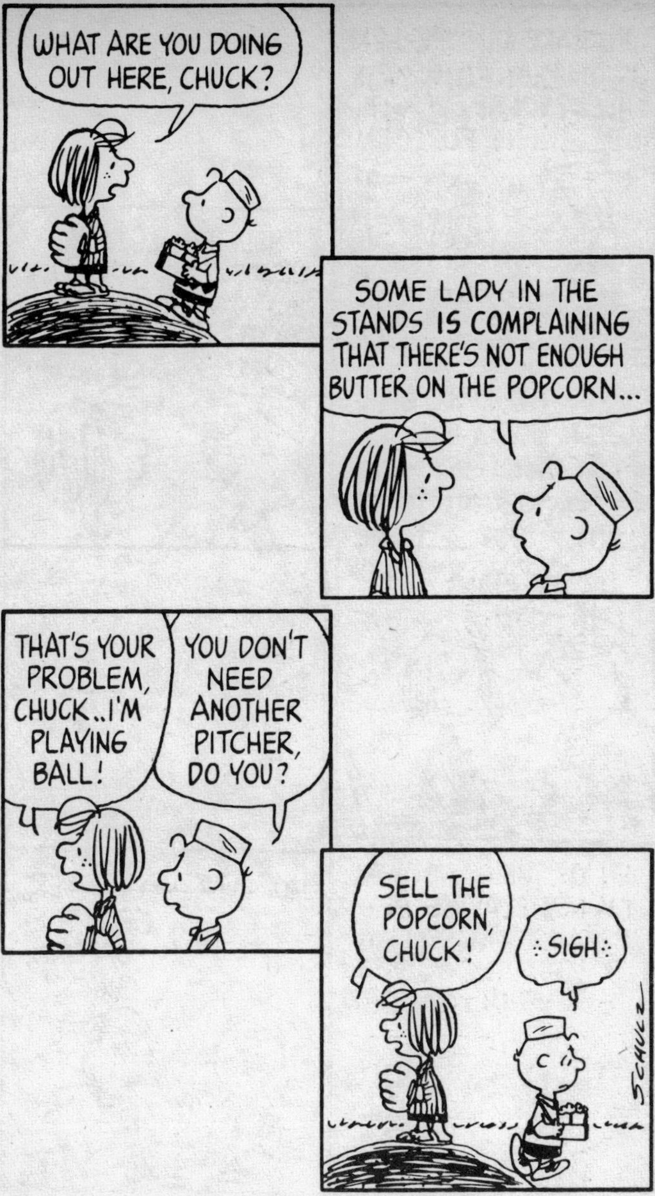
WHAT ARE YOU DOING OUT HERE, CHUCK?
SOME LADY IN THE STANDS IS COMPLAINING THAT THERE'S NOT ENOUGH BUTTER ON THE POPCORN...
THAT'S YOUR PROBLEM, CHUCK..I'M PLAYING BALL!
YOU DON'T NEED ANOTHER PITCHER, DO YOU?
SELL THE POPCORN, CHUCK!
SIGH
SCHULZ

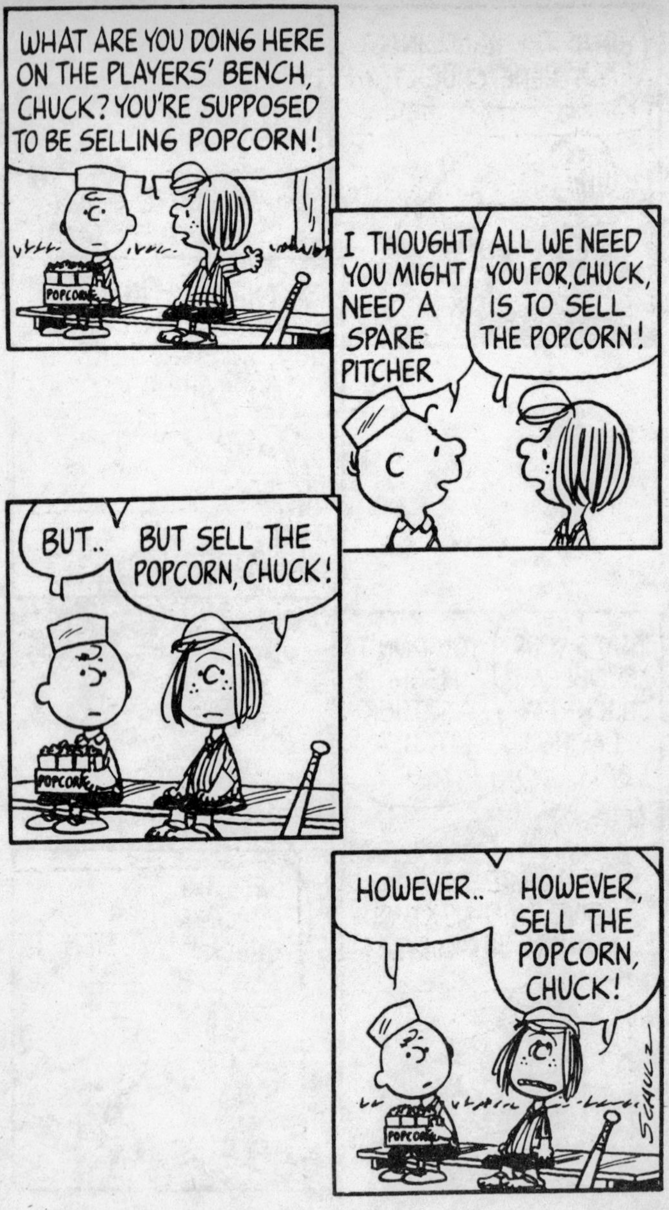
WHAT ARE YOU DOING HERE ON THE PLAYERS' BENCH, CHUCK? YOU'RE SUPPOSED TO BE SELLING POPCORN!
POPCORN
I THOUGHT YOU MIGHT NEED A SPARE PITCHER
ALL WE NEED YOU FOR, CHUCK, IS TO SELL THE POPCORN!
BUT..
BUT SELL THE POPCORN, CHUCK!
POPCORN
HOWEVER..
HOWEVER, SELL THE POPCORN, CHUCK!
POPCORN
SCHULZ

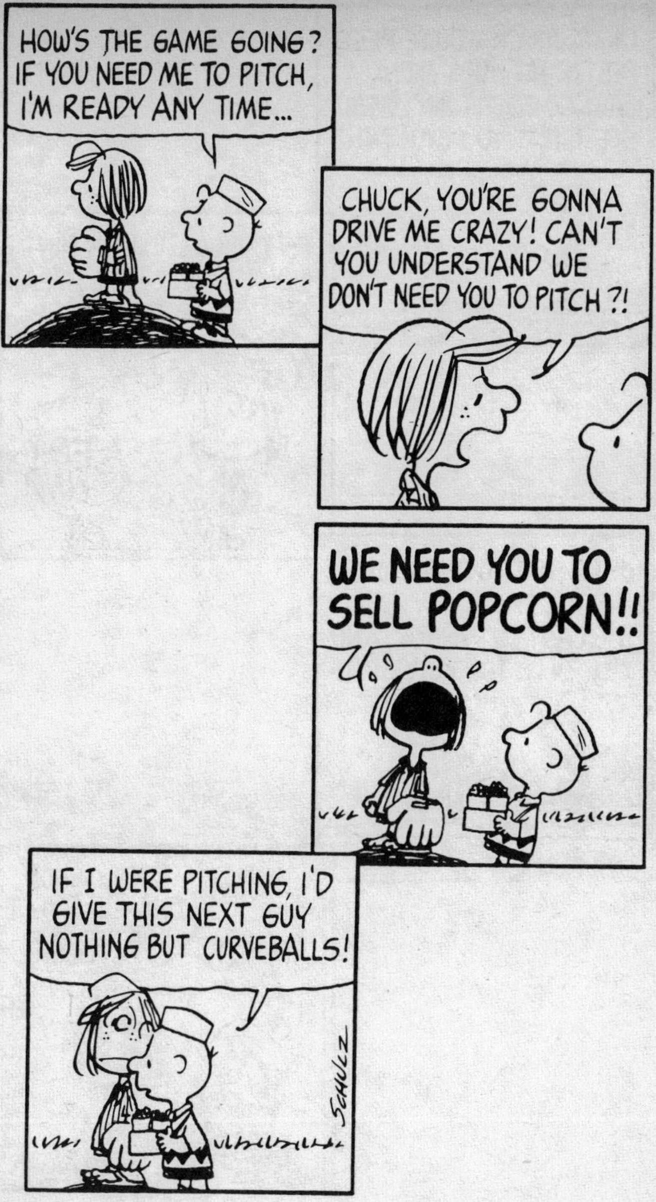
HOW'S THE GAME GOING? IF YOU NEED ME TO PITCH, I'M READY ANY TIME...
CHUCK, YOU'RE GONNA DRIVE ME CRAZY! CAN'T YOU UNDERSTAND WE DON'T NEED YOU TO PITCH ?!
WE NEED YOU TO SELL POPCORN!!
IF I WERE PITCHING, I'D GIVE THIS NEXT GUY NOTHING BUT CURVEBALLS!
SCHULZ

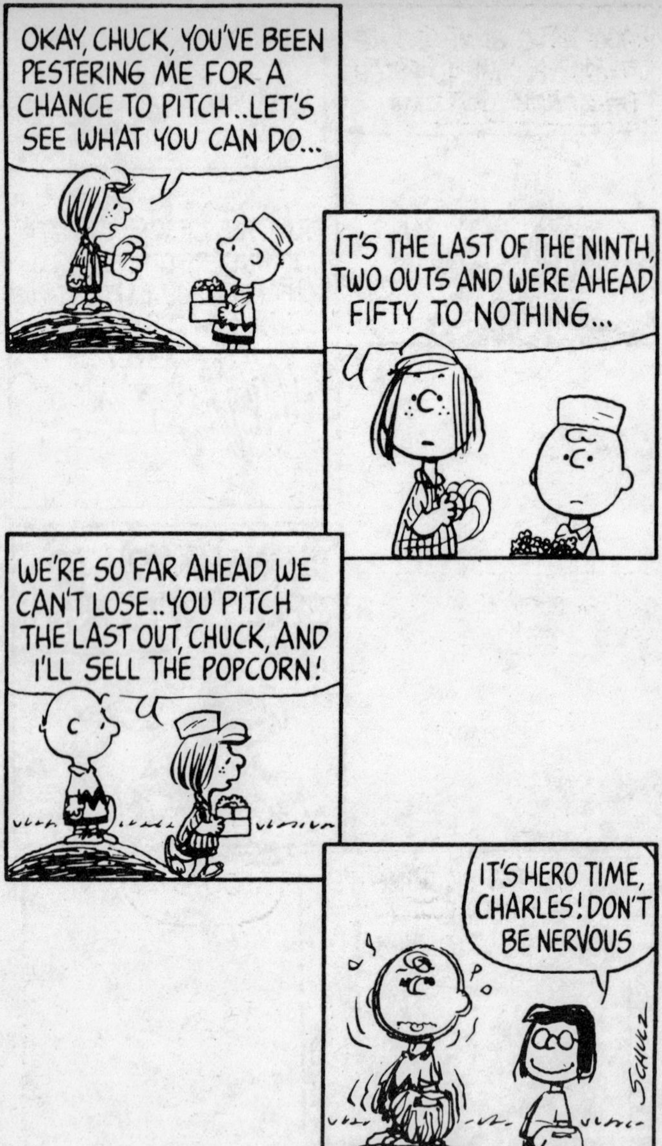
OKAY, CHUCK, YOU'VE BEEN PESTERING ME FOR A CHANCE TO PITCH..LET'S SEE WHAT YOU CAN DO...
IT'S THE LAST OF THE NINTH, TWO OUTS AND WE'RE AHEAD FIFTY TO NOTHING...
WE'RE SO FAR AHEAD WE CAN'T LOSE..YOU PITCH THE LAST OUT, CHUCK, AND I'LL SELL THE POPCORN!
IT'S HERO TIME, CHARLES! DON'T BE NERVOUS
SCHULZ

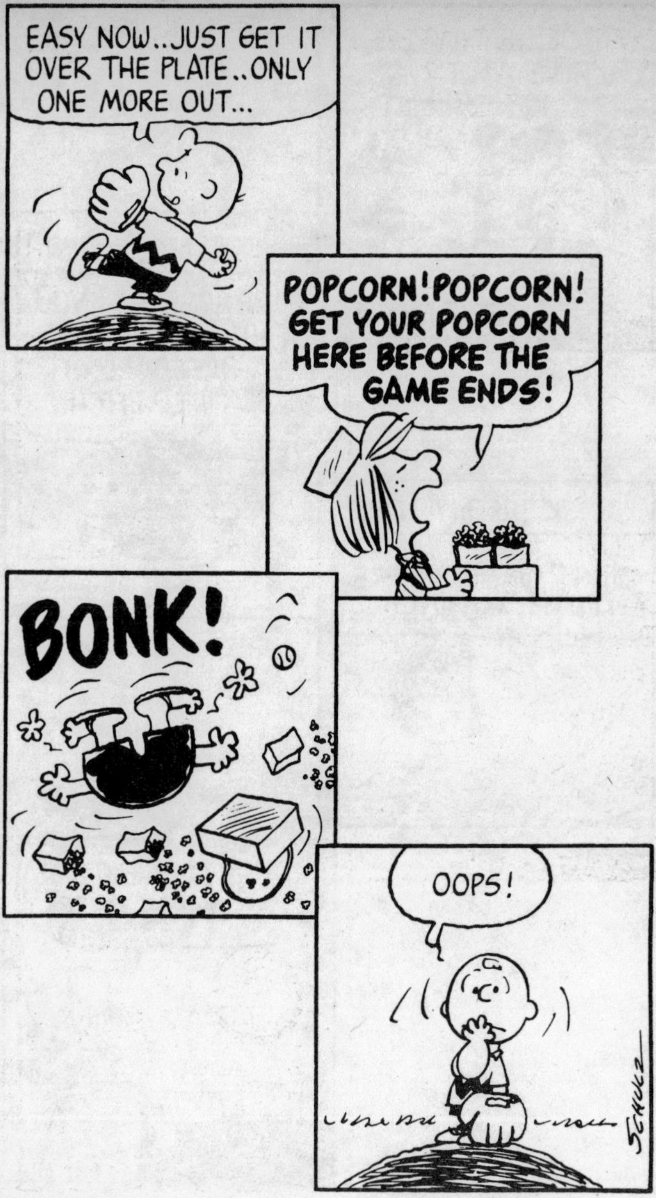
EASY NOW..JUST GET IT OVER THE PLATE..ONLY ONE MORE OUT...
POPCORN! POPCORN! GET YOUR POPCORN HERE BEFORE THE GAME ENDS!
BONK!
OOPS!
SCHULZ

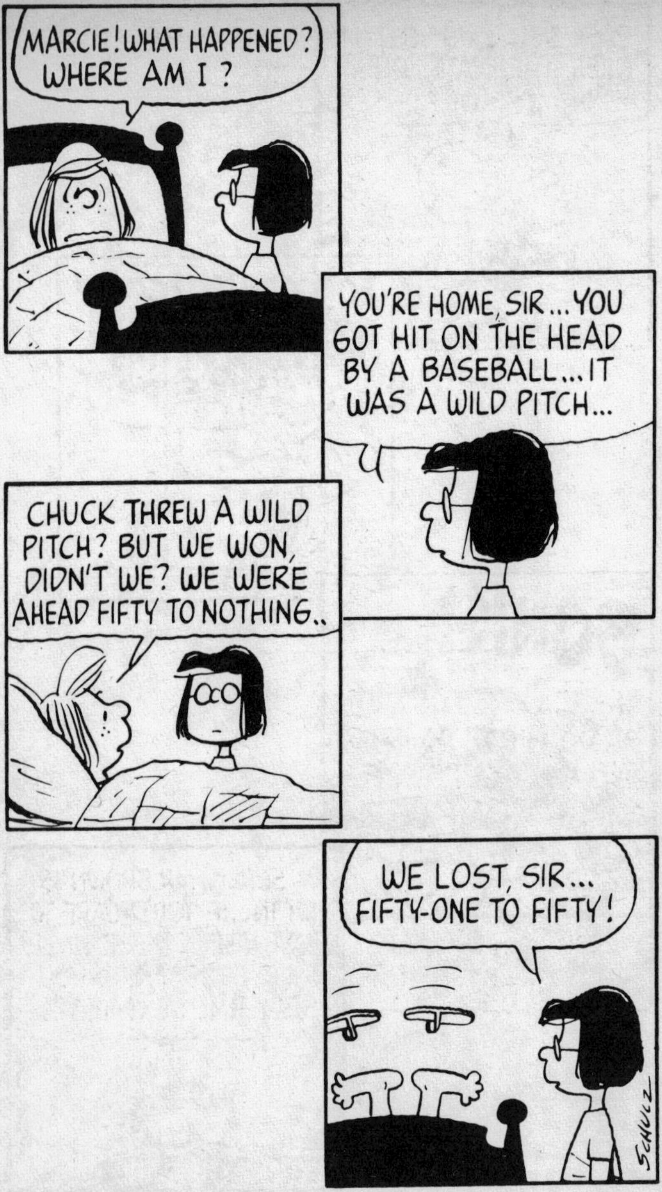
MARCIE! WHAT HAPPENED? WHERE AM I?
YOU'RE HOME, SIR... YOU GOT HIT ON THE HEAD BY A BASEBALL... IT WAS A WILD PITCH...
CHUCK THREW A WILD PITCH? BUT WE WON, DIDN'T WE? WE WERE AHEAD FIFTY TO NOTHING..
WE LOST, SIR... FIFTY-ONE TO FIFTY!
SCHULZ

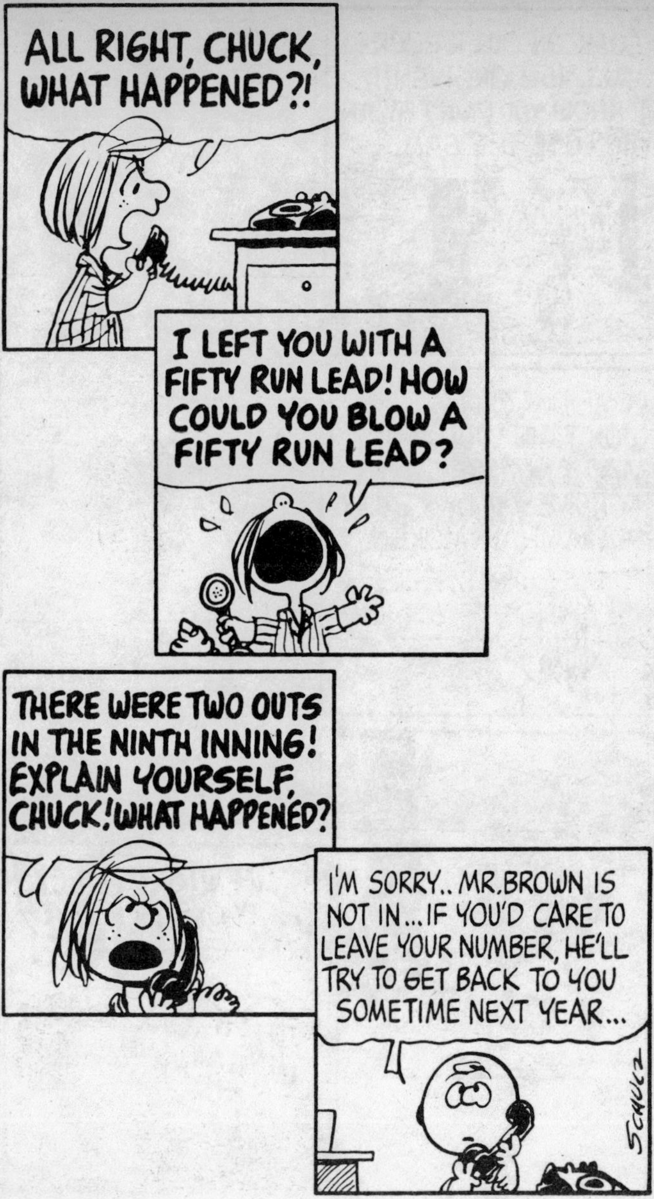
ALL RIGHT, CHUCK, WHAT HAPPENED?!
I LEFT YOU WITH A FIFTY RUN LEAD! HOW COULD YOU BLOW A FIFTY RUN LEAD?
THERE WERE TWO OUTS IN THE NINTH INNING! EXPLAIN YOURSELF, CHUCK! WHAT HAPPENED?
I'M SORRY.. MR. BROWN IS NOT IN... IF YOU'D CARE TO LEAVE YOUR NUMBER, HE'LL TRY TO GET BACK TO YOU SOMETIME NEXT YEAR...
SCHULZ

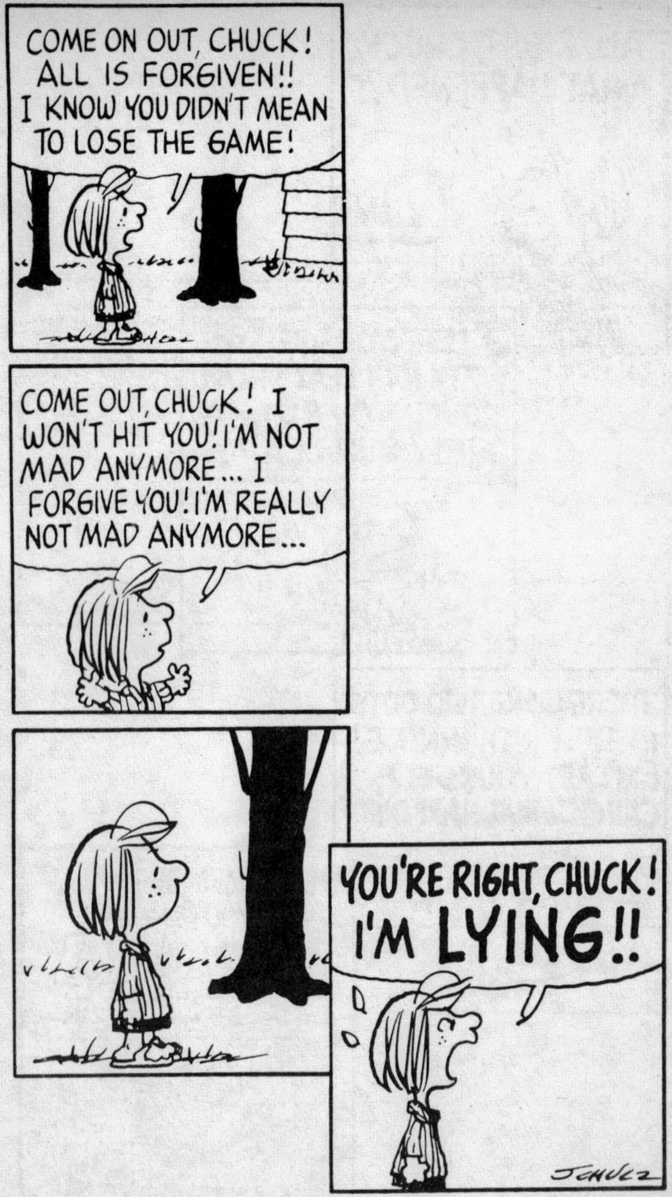
COME ON OUT, CHUCK! ALL IS FORGIVEN!! I KNOW YOU DIDN'T MEAN TO LOSE THE GAME!
COME OUT, CHUCK! I WON'T HIT YOU! I'M NOT MAD ANYMORE... I FORGIVE YOU! I'M REALLY NOT MAD ANYMORE...
YOU'RE RIGHT, CHUCK! I'M LYING!!
SCHULZ

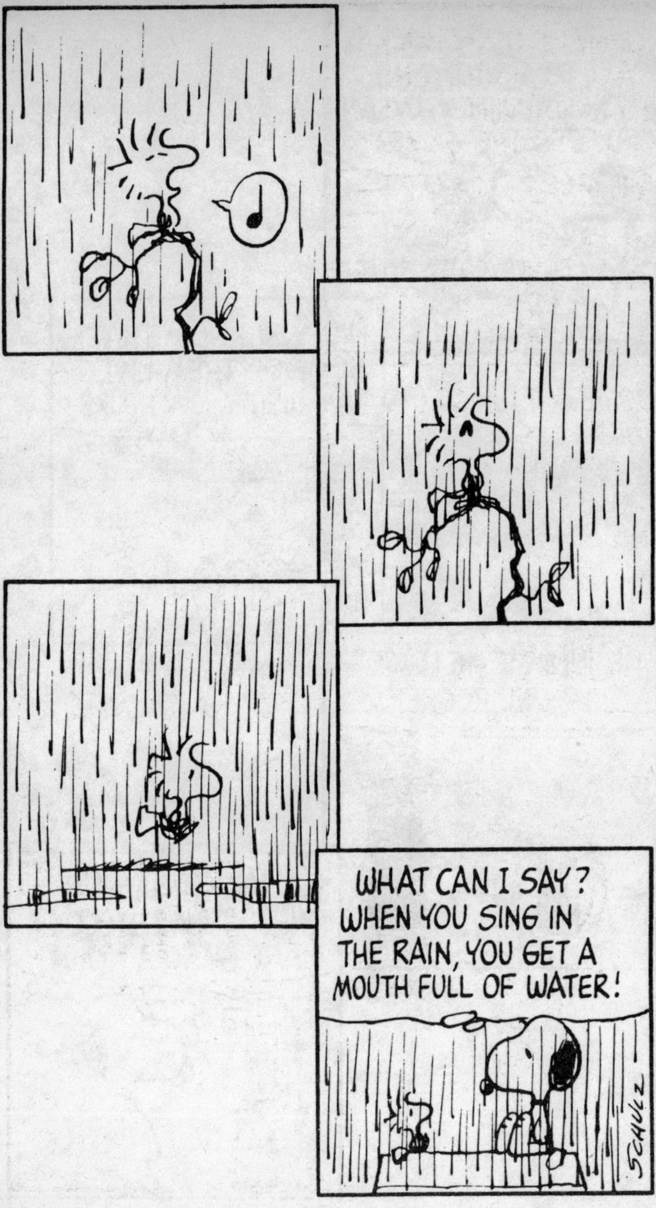
WHAT CAN I SAY? WHEN YOU SING IN THE RAIN, YOU GET A MOUTH FULL OF WATER!
SCHULZ

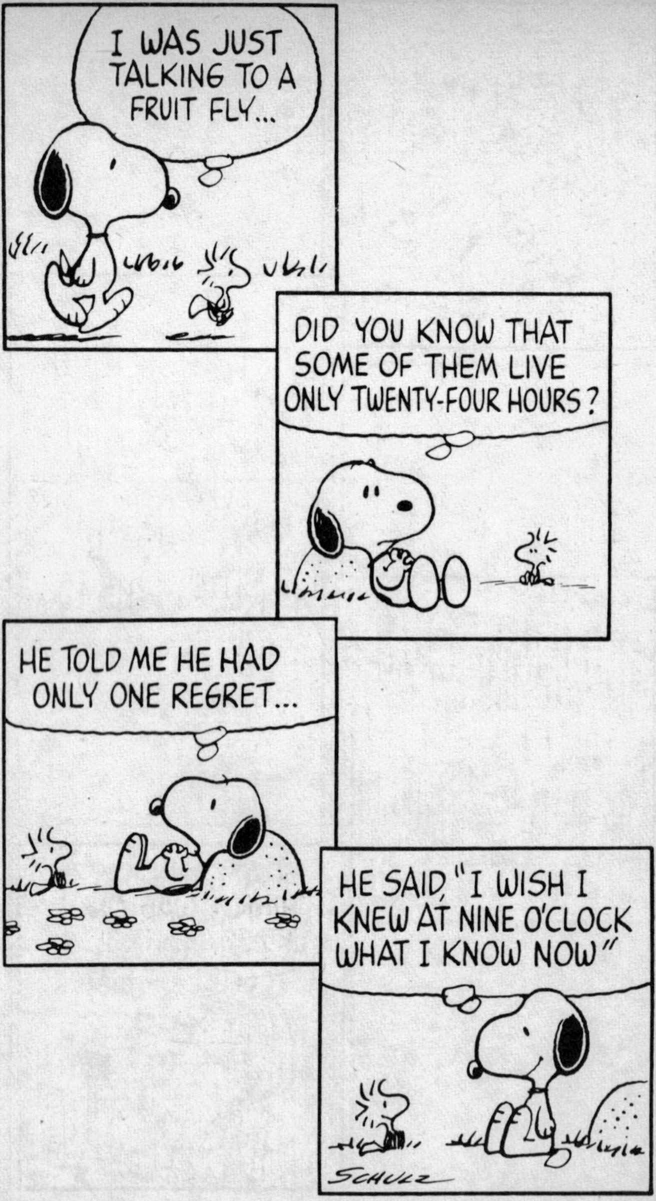
I WAS JUST TALKING TO A FRUIT FLY...
DID YOU KNOW THAT SOME OF THEM LIVE ONLY TWENTY-FOUR HOURS?
HE TOLD ME HE HAD ONLY ONE REGRET...
HE SAID, "I WISH I KNEW AT NINE O'CLOCK WHAT I KNOW NOW"
SCHULZ

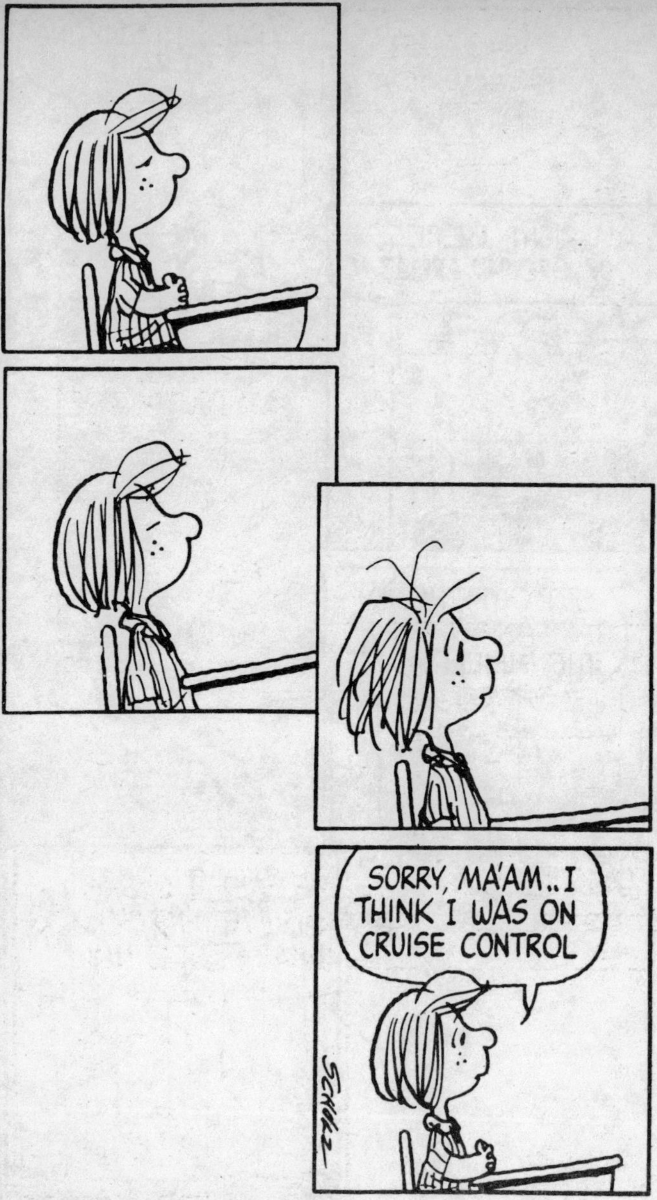
SORRY, MA'AM..I THINK I WAS ON CRUISE CONTROL
SCHULZ

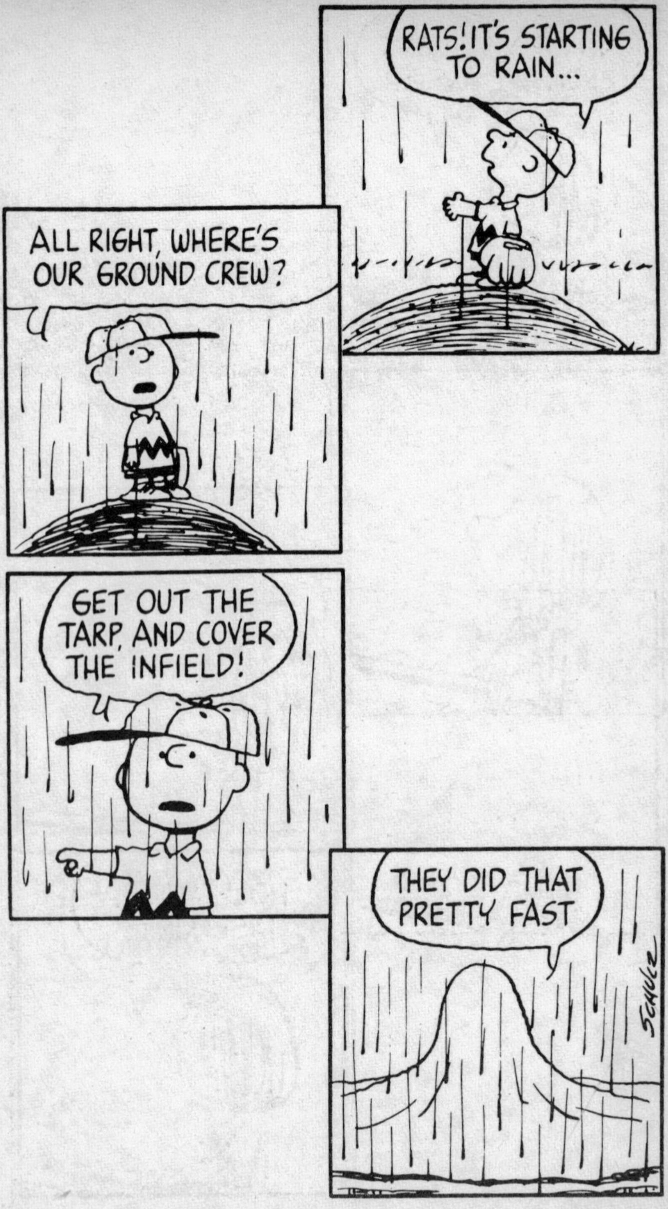
RATS! IT'S STARTING TO RAIN...
ALL RIGHT, WHERE'S OUR GROUND CREW?
GET OUT THE TARP, AND COVER THE INFIELD!
THEY DID THAT PRETTY FAST
SCHULZ

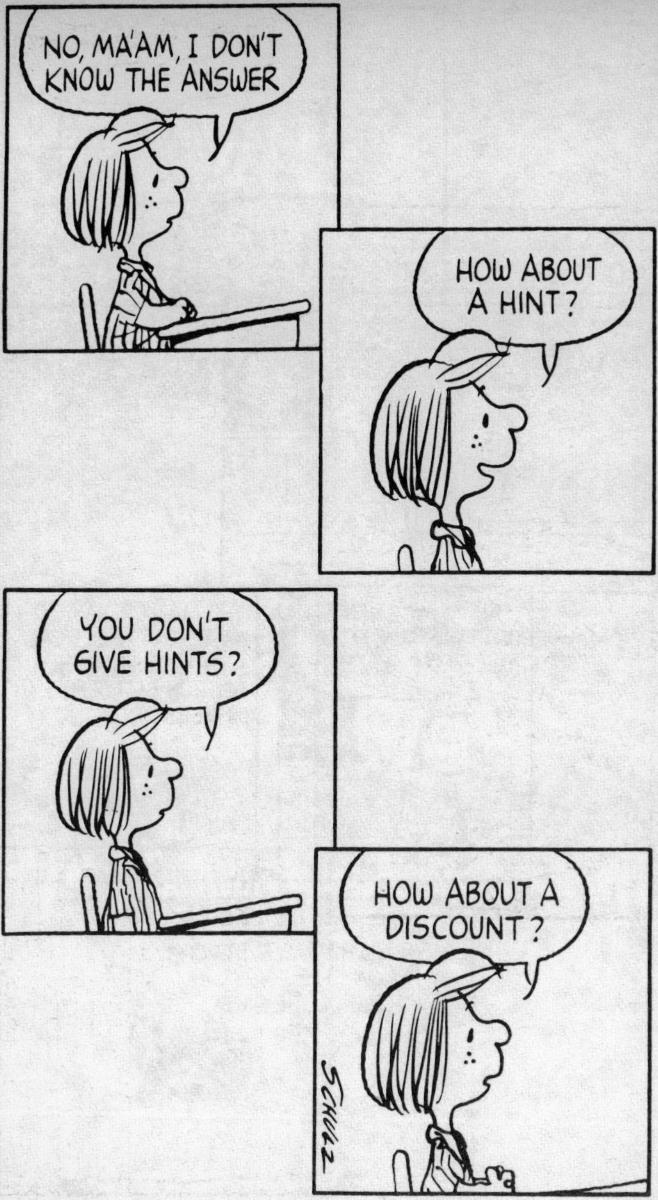
NO, MA'AM, I DON'T KNOW THE ANSWER
HOW ABOUT A HINT?
YOU DON'T GIVE HINTS?
HOW ABOUT A DISCOUNT?
SCHULZ

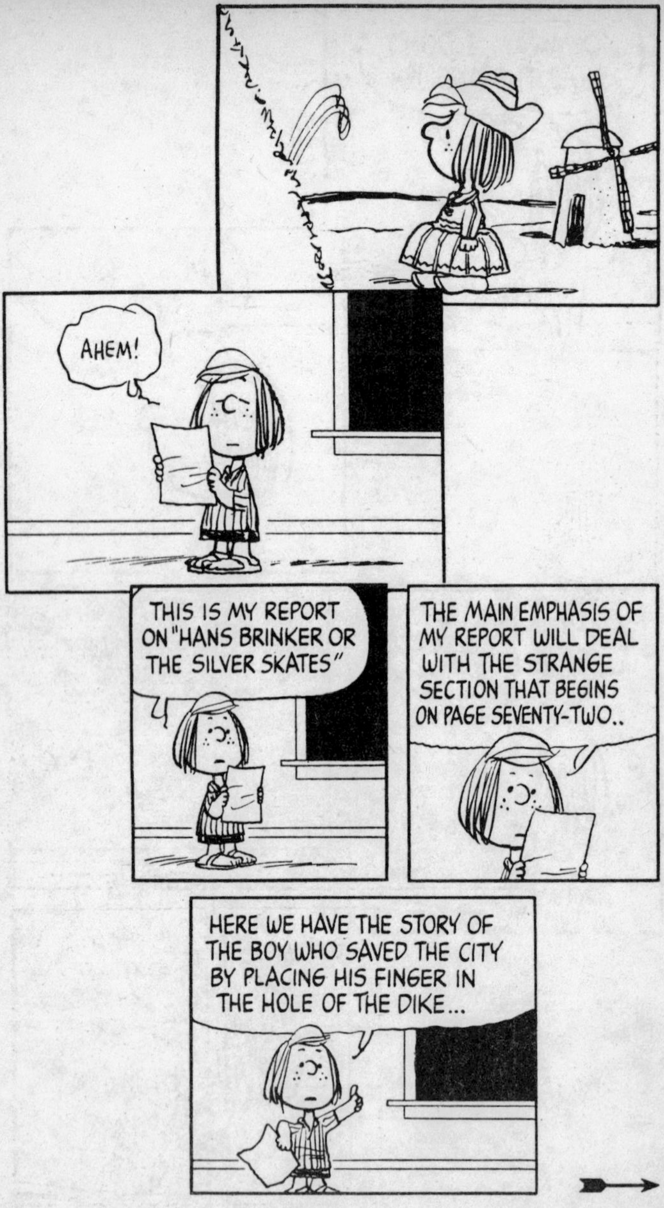
AHEM!
THIS IS MY REPORT ON "HANS BRINKER OR THE SILVER SKATES"
THE MAIN EMPHASIS OF MY REPORT WILL DEAL WITH THE STRANGE SECTION THAT BEGINS ON PAGE SEVENTY-TWO..
HERE WE HAVE THE STORY OF THE BOY WHO SAVED THE CITY BY PLACING HIS FINGER IN THE HOLE OF THE DIKE...

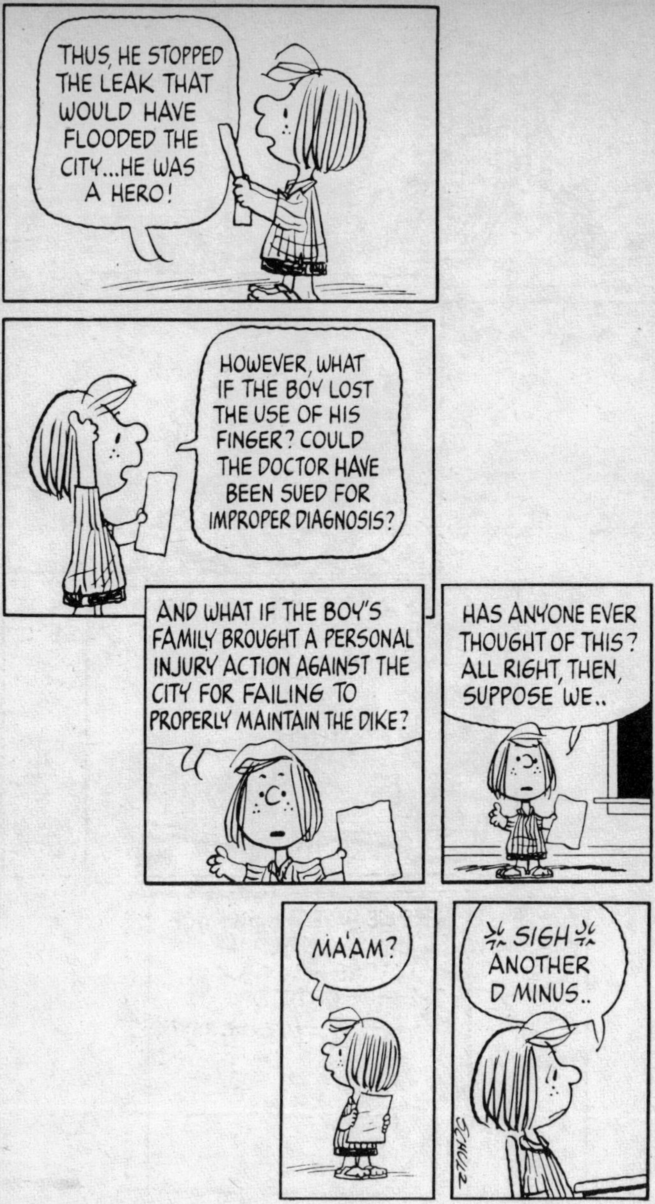
THUS, HE STOPPED THE LEAK THAT WOULD HAVE FLOODED THE CITY...HE WAS A HERO!
HOWEVER, WHAT IF THE BOY LOST THE USE OF HIS FINGER? COULD THE DOCTOR HAVE BEEN SUED FOR IMPROPER DIAGNOSIS?
AND WHAT IF THE BOY'S FAMILY BROUGHT A PERSONAL INJURY ACTION AGAINST THE CITY FOR FAILING TO PROPERLY MAINTAIN THE DIKE?
HAS ANYONE EVER THOUGHT OF THIS? ALL RIGHT, THEN, SUPPOSE WE..
MA'AM?
SIGH
ANOTHER D MINUS..
SCHULZ

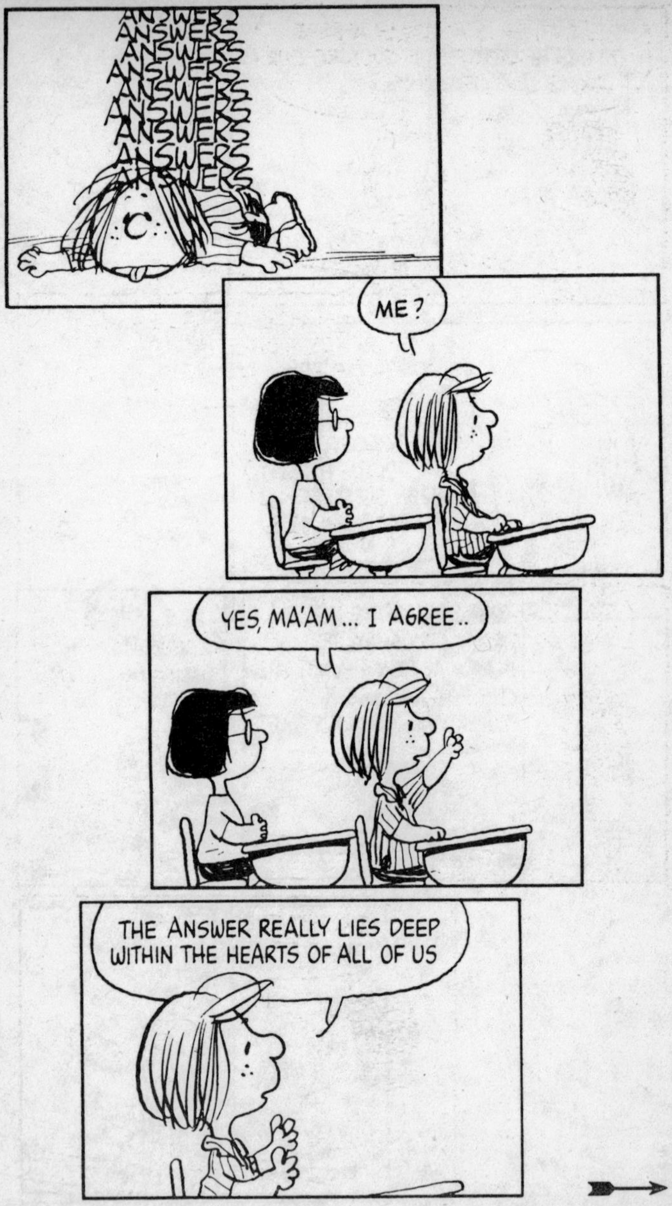
ANSWERS ANSWERS ANSWERS ANSWERS ANSWERS ANSWERS ANSWERS ANSWERS ANSWERS
ME ?
YES, MA'AM ... I AGREE ..
THE ANSWER REALLY LIES DEEP WITHIN THE HEARTS OF ALL OF US

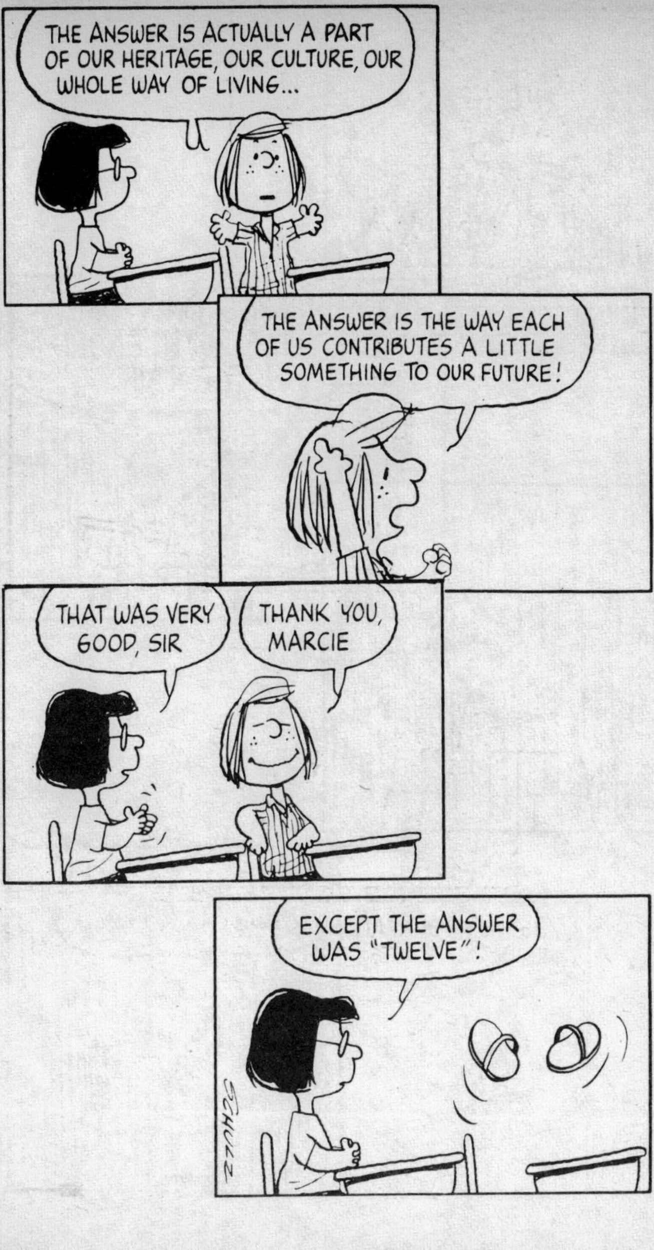
THE ANSWER IS ACTUALLY A PART OF OUR HERITAGE, OUR CULTURE, OUR WHOLE WAY OF LIVING...
THE ANSWER IS THE WAY EACH OF US CONTRIBUTES A LITTLE SOMETHING TO OUR FUTURE!
THAT WAS VERY GOOD, SIR
THANK YOU, MARCIE
EXCEPT THE ANSWER WAS "TWELVE"!
SCHULZ

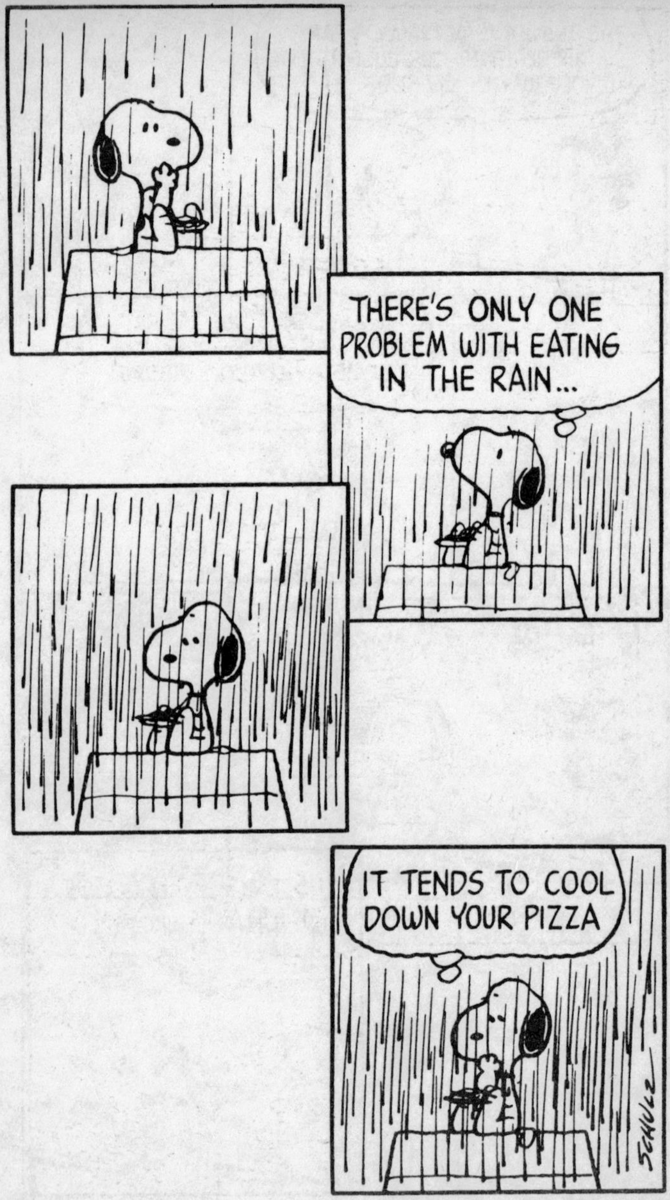
THERE'S ONLY ONE PROBLEM WITH EATING IN THE RAIN...
IT TENDS TO COOL DOWN YOUR PIZZA
SCHULZ

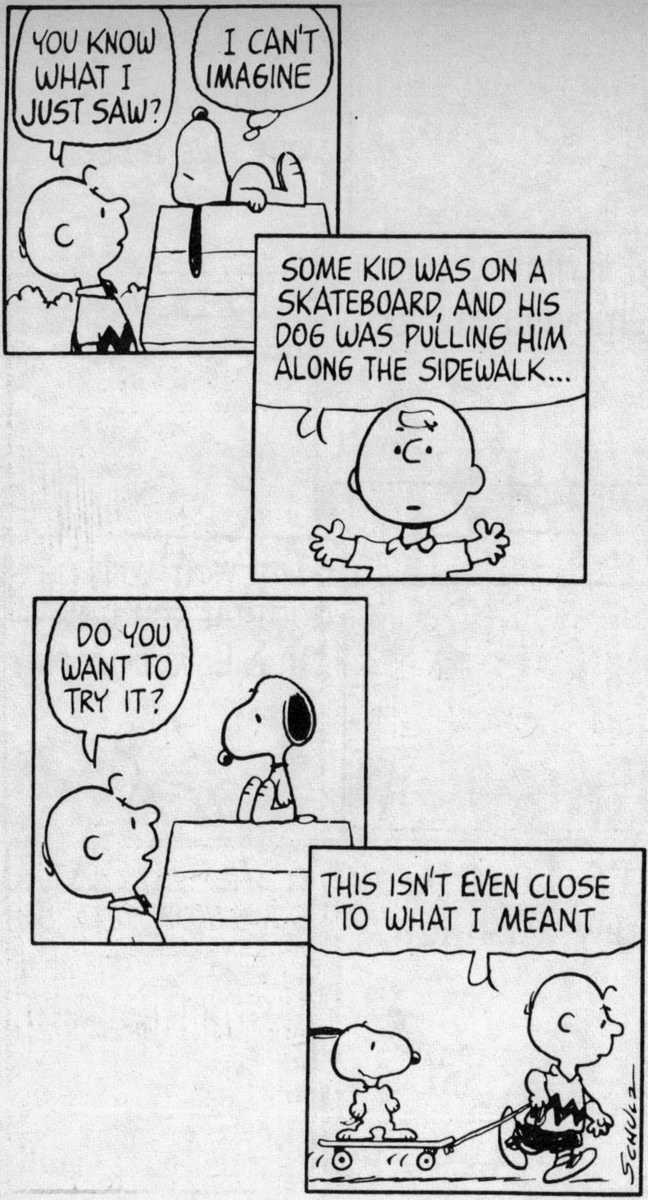
YOU KNOW WHAT I JUST SAW?
I CAN'T IMAGINE
SOME KID WAS ON A SKATEBOARD, AND HIS DOG WAS PULLING HIM ALONG THE SIDEWALK...
DO YOU WANT TO TRY IT?
THIS ISN'T EVEN CLOSE TO WHAT I MEANT
SCHULZ

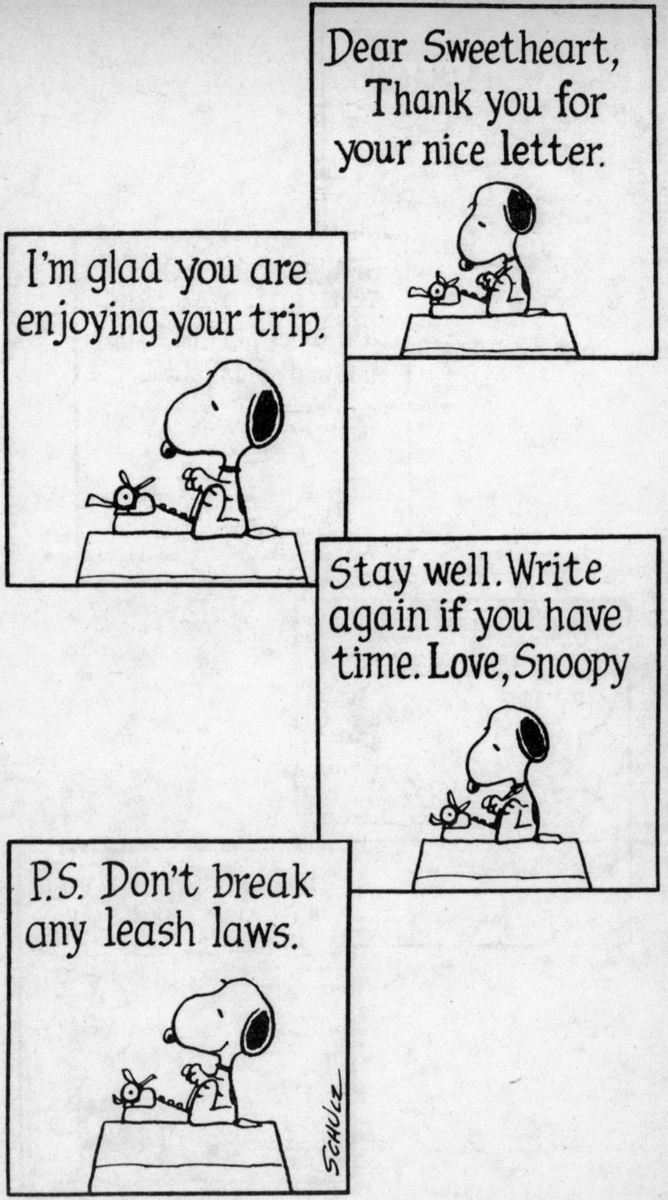
Dear Sweetheart,
Thank you for your nice letter.
I'm glad you are enjoying your trip.
Stay well. Write again if you have time. Love, Snoopy
P.S. Don't break any leash laws.
SCHULZ

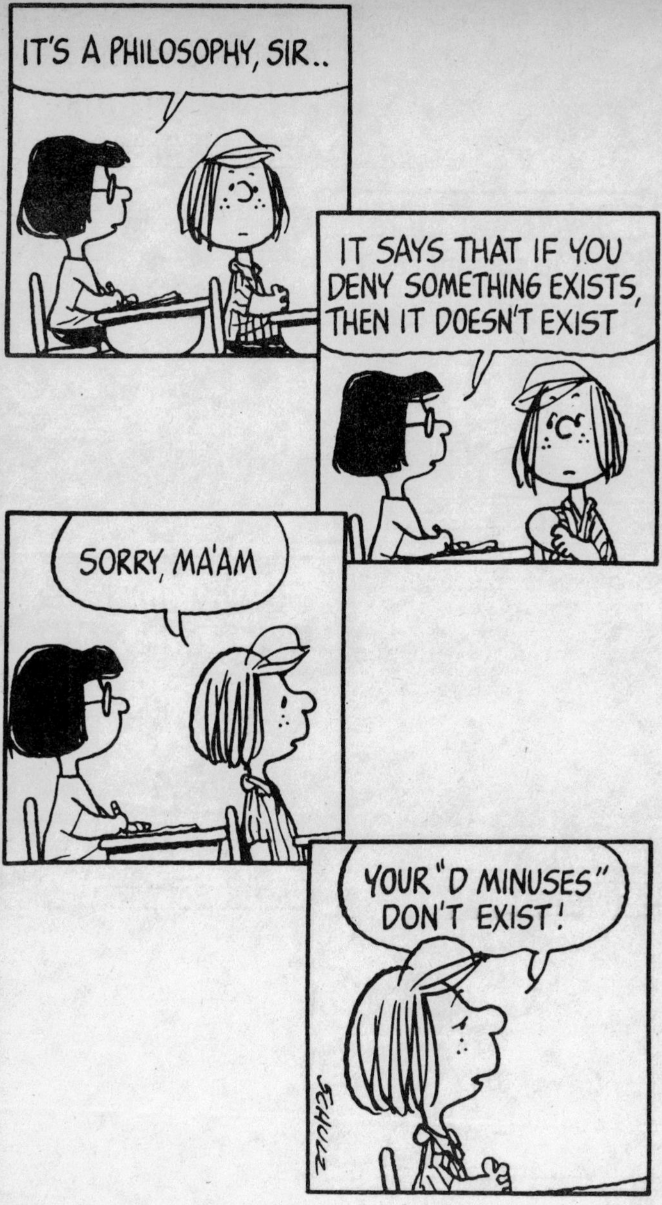
IT'S A PHILOSOPHY, SIR..
IT SAYS THAT IF YOU DENY SOMETHING EXISTS, THEN IT DOESN'T EXIST
SORRY, MA'AM
YOUR "D MINUSES" DON'T EXIST!
SCHULZ

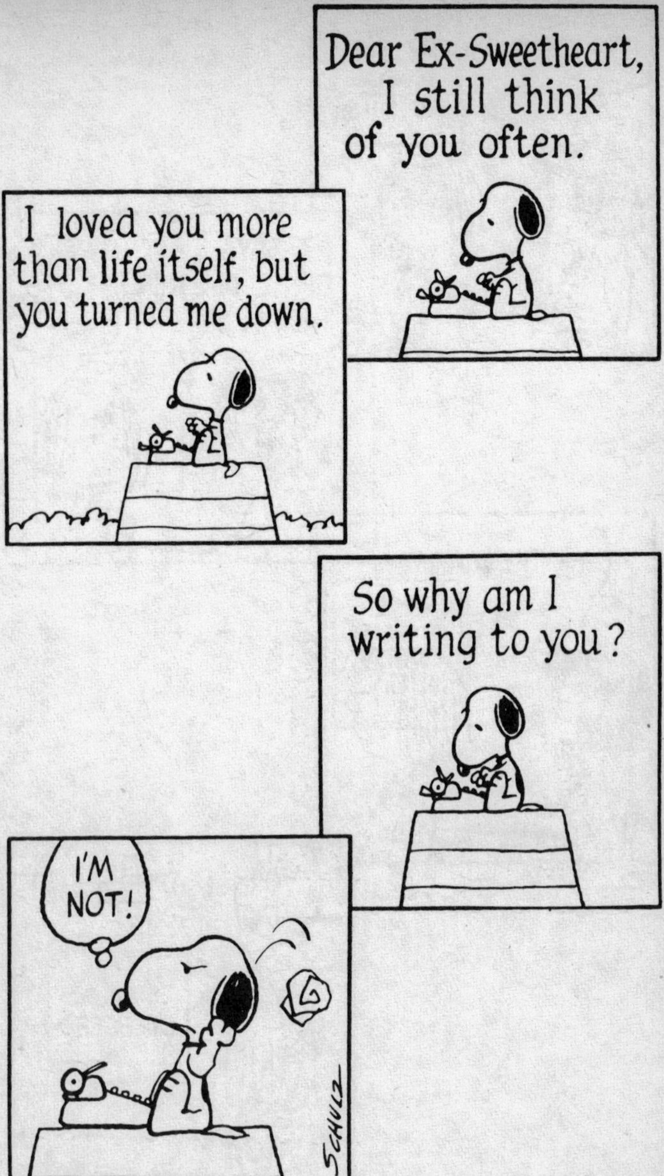

Dear Ex-Sweetheart,
I still think of you often.
I loved you more than life itself, but you turned me down.
So why am I writing to you?
I'M NOT!
SCHULZ

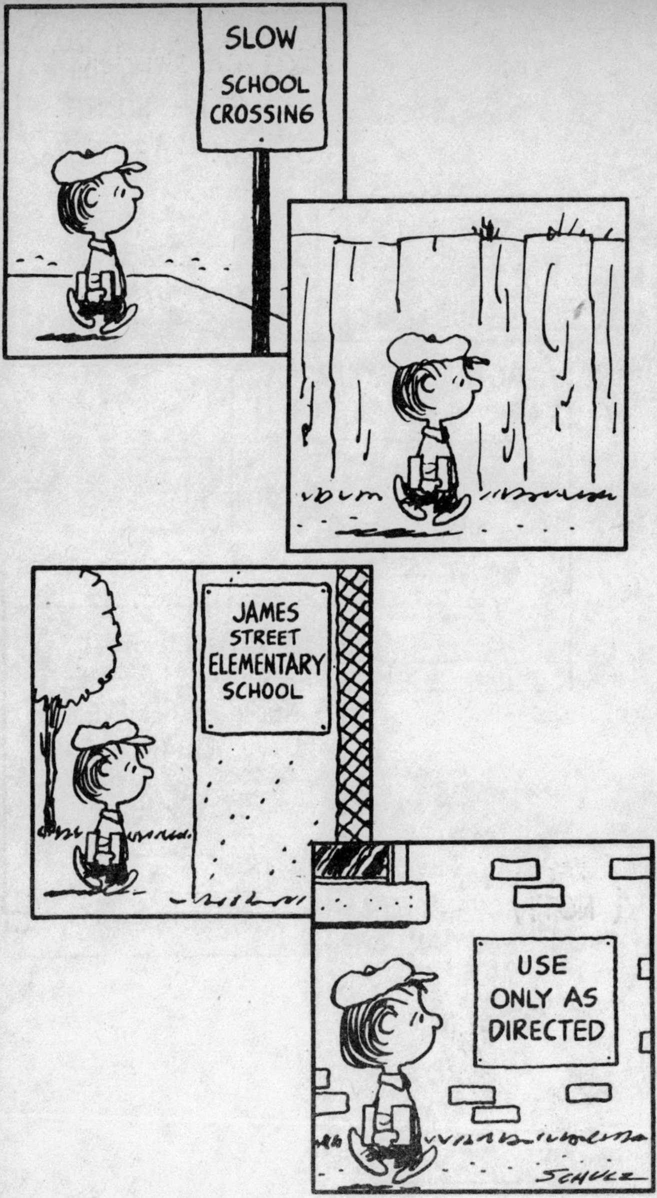
SLOW
SCHOOL CROSSING
JAMES STREET ELEMENTARY SCHOOL
USE ONLY AS DIRECTED
SCHULZ

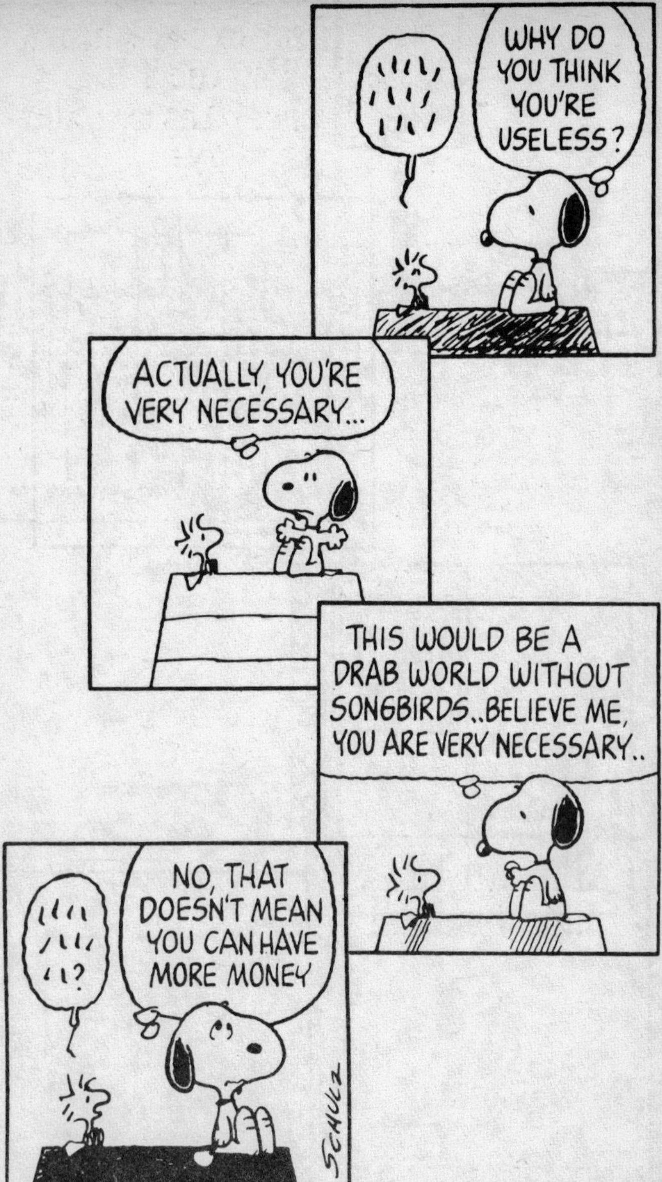
WHY DO YOU THINK YOU'RE USELESS?
ACTUALLY, YOU'RE VERY NECESSARY...
THIS WOULD BE A DRAB WORLD WITHOUT SONGBIRDS..BELIEVE ME, YOU ARE VERY NECESSARY..
NO, THAT DOESN'T MEAN YOU CAN HAVE MORE MONEY
SCHULZ

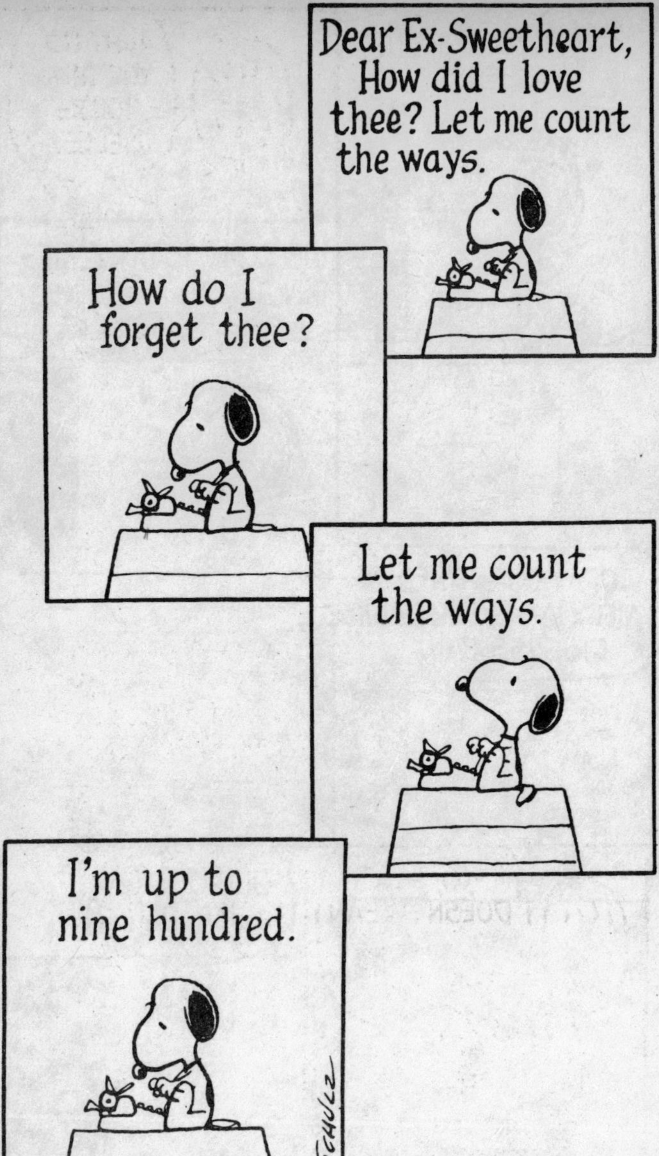
Dear Ex-Sweetheart,
How did I love thee? Let me count the ways.
How do I forget thee?
Let me count the ways.
I'm up to nine hundred.
SCHULZ

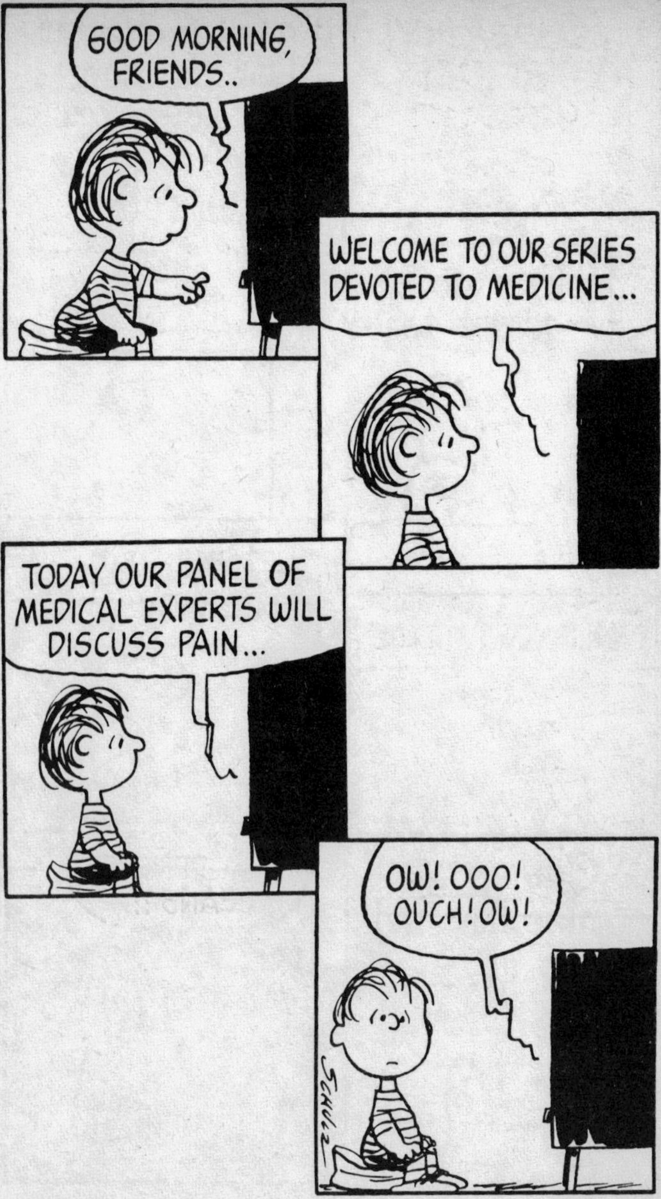
GOOD MORNING, FRIENDS..
WELCOME TO OUR SERIES DEVOTED TO MEDICINE...
TODAY OUR PANEL OF MEDICAL EXPERTS WILL DISCUSS PAIN...
OW! OOO! OUCH! OW!
SCHULZ

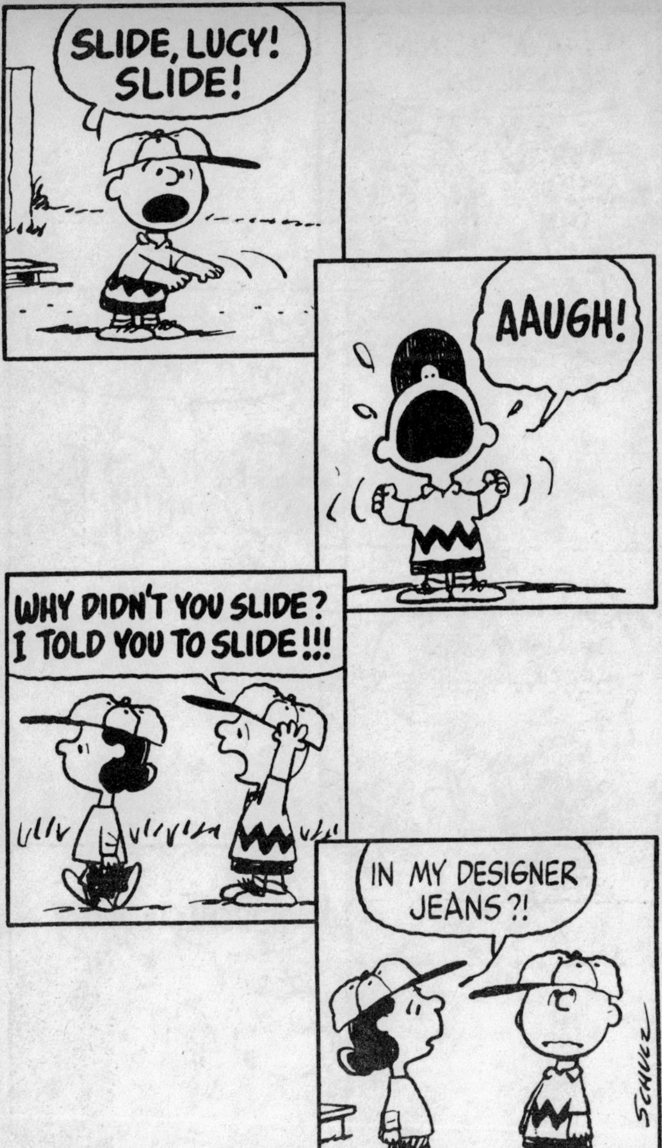
SLIDE, LUCY! SLIDE!
AAUGH!
WHY DIDN'T YOU SLIDE? I TOLD YOU TO SLIDE!!!
IN MY DESIGNER JEANS?!
SCHULZ

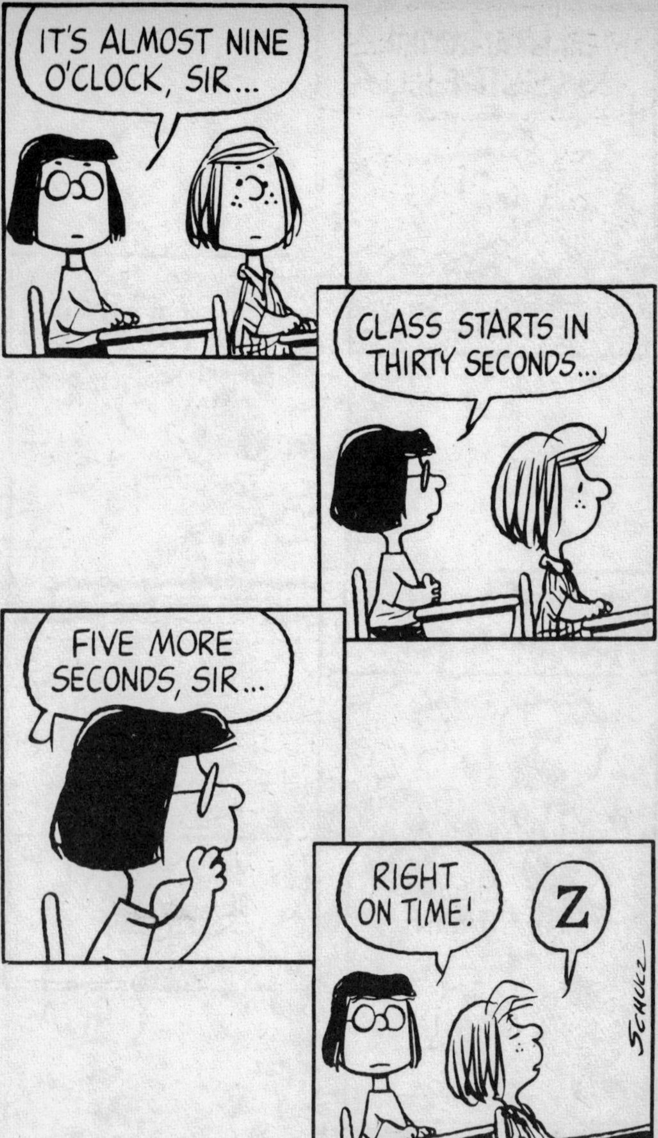
IT'S ALMOST NINE O'CLOCK, SIR...
CLASS STARTS IN THIRTY SECONDS...
FIVE MORE SECONDS, SIR...
RIGHT ON TIME!
Z
SCHULZ

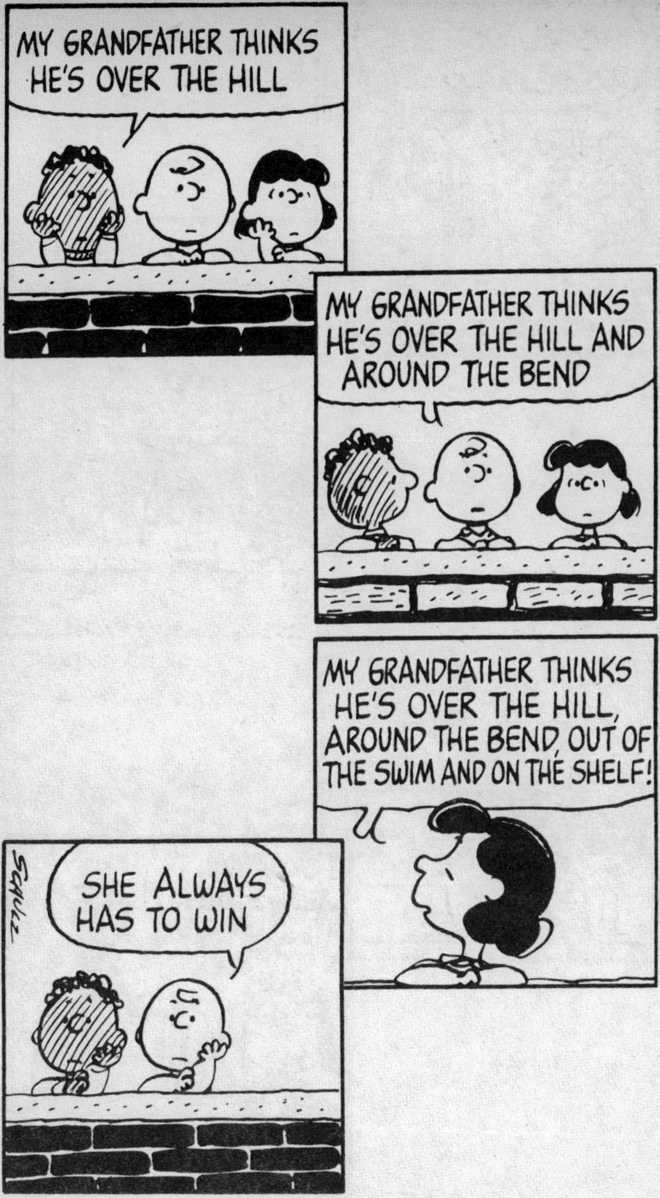
MY GRANDFATHER THINKS HE'S OVER THE HILL
MY GRANDFATHER THINKS HE'S OVER THE HILL AND AROUND THE BEND
MY GRANDFATHER THINKS HE'S OVER THE HILL, AROUND THE BEND, OUT OF THE SWIM AND ON THE SHELF!
SCHULZ
SHE ALWAYS HAS TO WIN

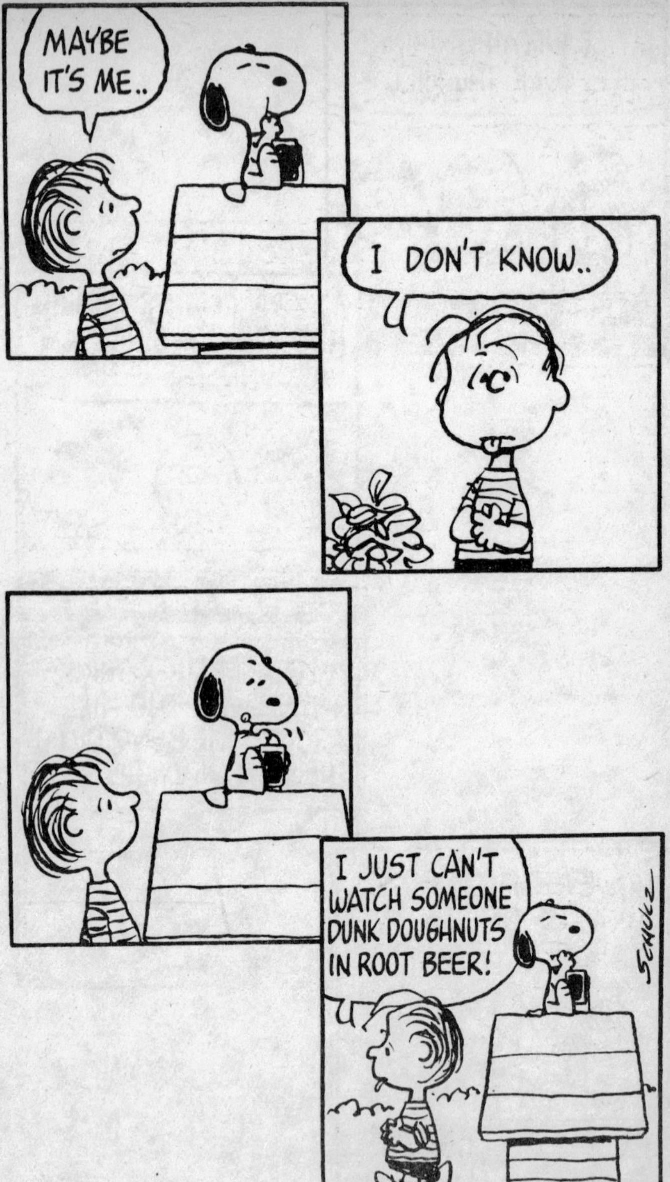
MAYBE IT'S ME..
I DON'T KNOW..
I JUST CAN'T WATCH SOMEONE DUNK DOUGHNUTS IN ROOT BEER!
SCHULZ

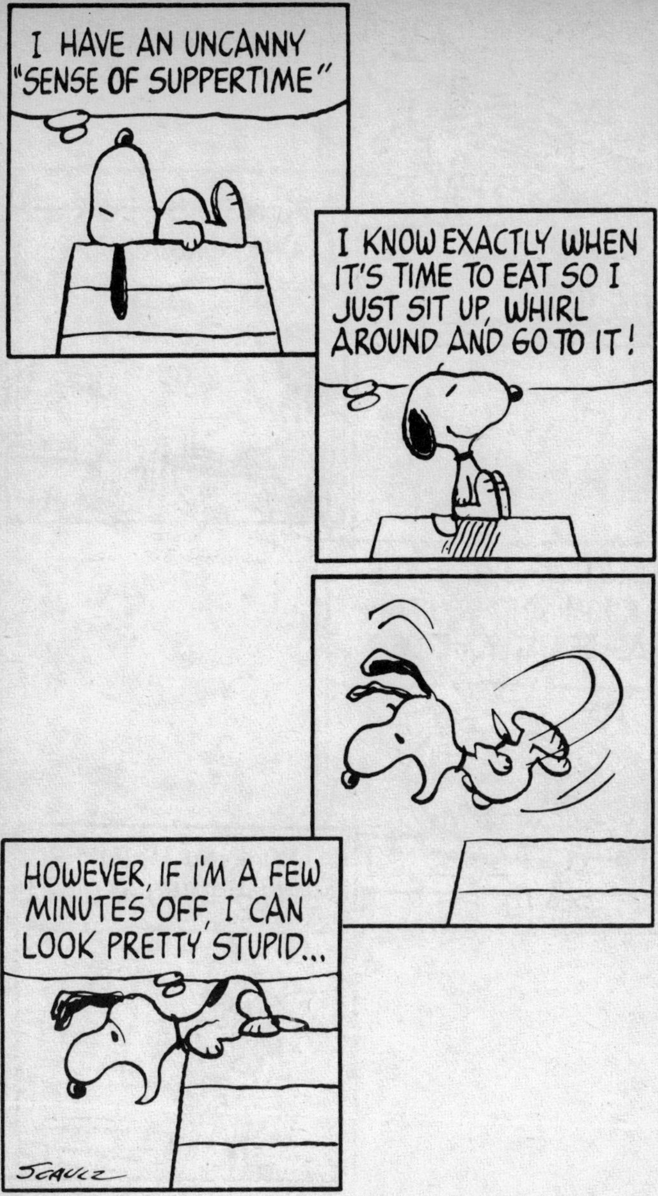
I HAVE AN UNCANNY "SENSE OF SUPPERTIME"
I KNOW EXACTLY WHEN IT'S TIME TO EAT SO I JUST SIT UP, WHIRL AROUND AND GO TO IT!
HOWEVER, IF I'M A FEW MINUTES OFF, I CAN LOOK PRETTY STUPID...

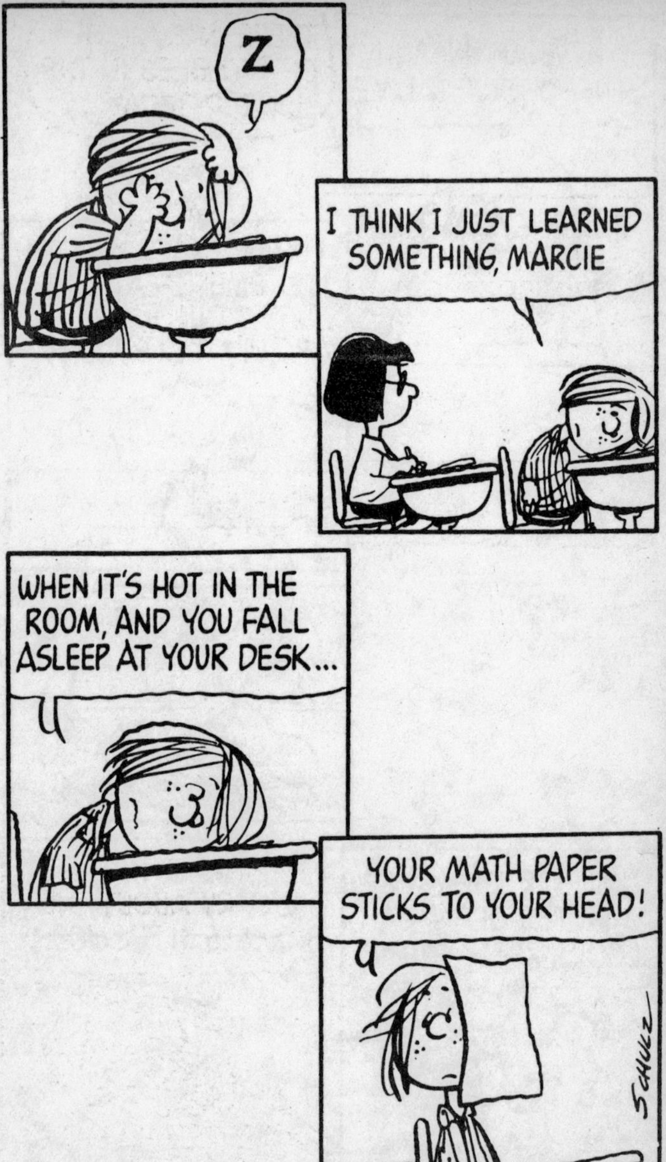
Z
I THINK I JUST LEARNED SOMETHING, MARCIE
WHEN IT'S HOT IN THE ROOM, AND YOU FALL ASLEEP AT YOUR DESK...
YOUR MATH PAPER STICKS TO YOUR HEAD!
SCHULZ

THERE ARE A LOT OF TROUBLES IN THE WORLD TODAY...
PLAYING BASEBALL HELPS TO TAKE YOUR MIND OFF THEM
POW!
I THINK I'D RATHER WORRY ABOUT THE TROUBLES IN THE WORLD
SCHULZ

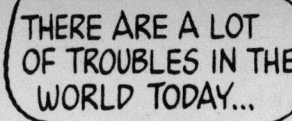

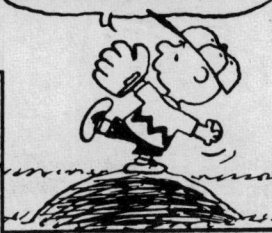

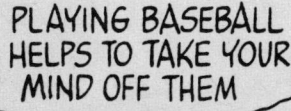

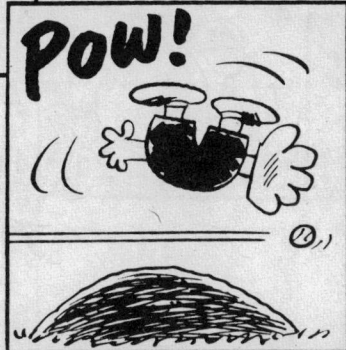

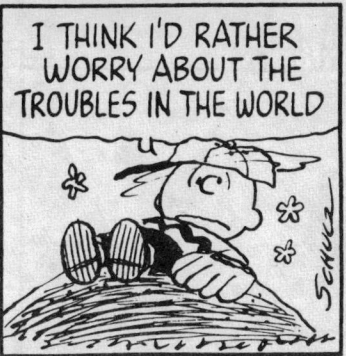

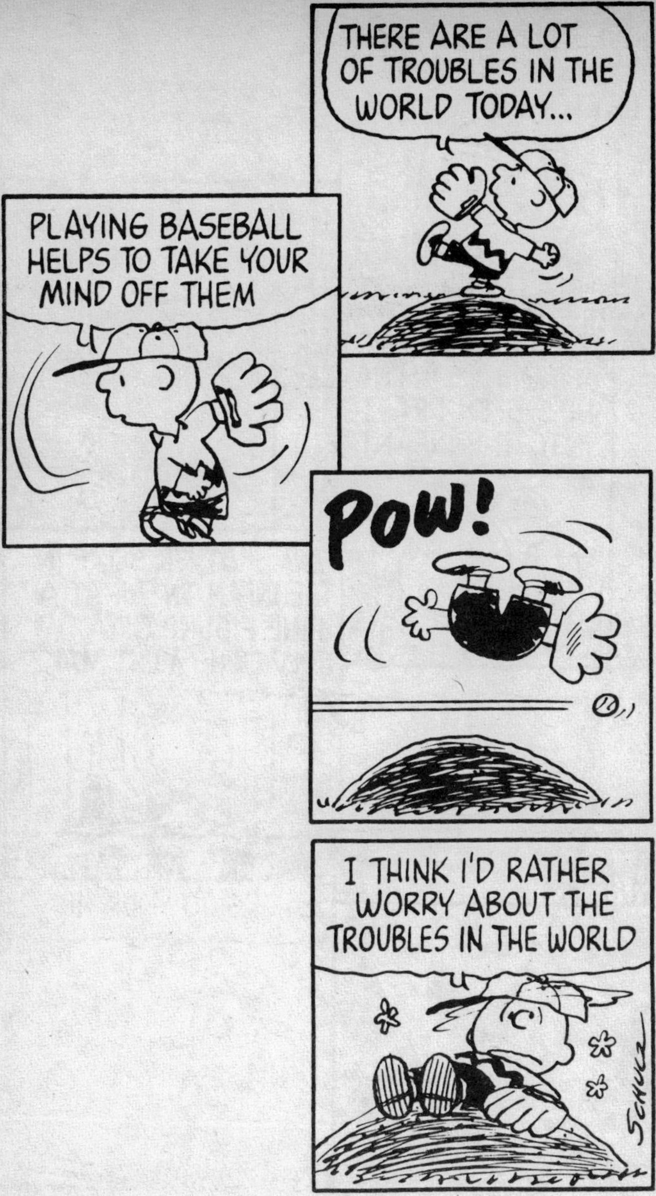

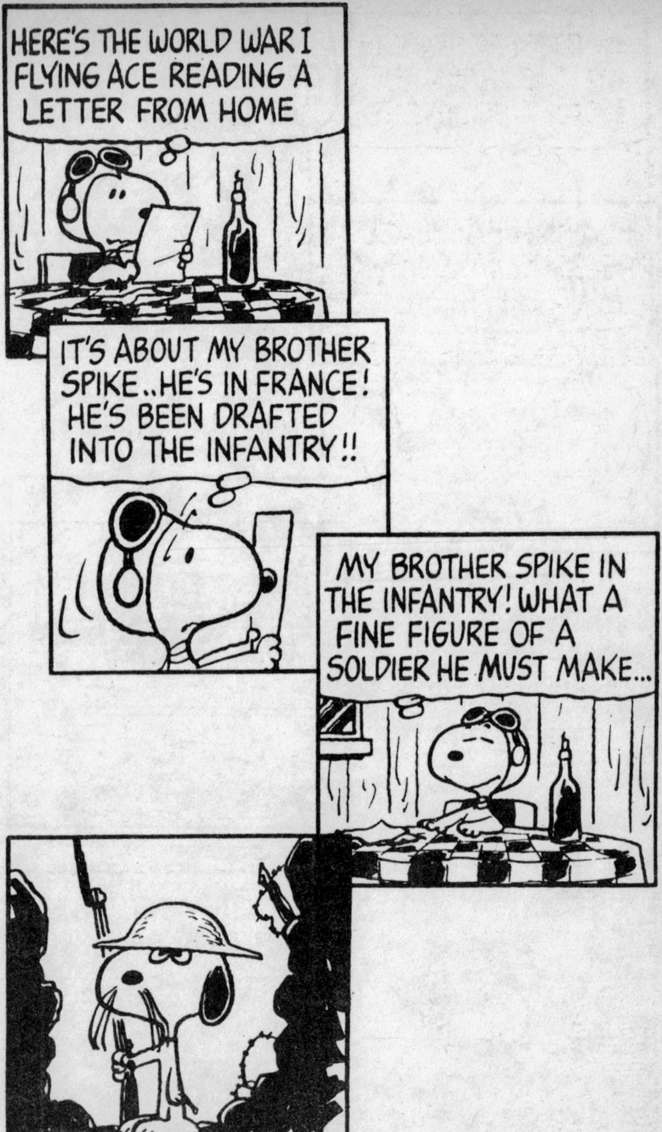
HERE'S THE WORLD WAR I FLYING ACE READING A LETTER FROM HOME
IT'S ABOUT MY BROTHER SPIKE..HE'S IN FRANCE! HE'S BEEN DRAFTED INTO THE INFANTRY!!
MY BROTHER SPIKE IN THE INFANTRY! WHAT A FINE FIGURE OF A SOLDIER HE MUST MAKE...
SCHULZ

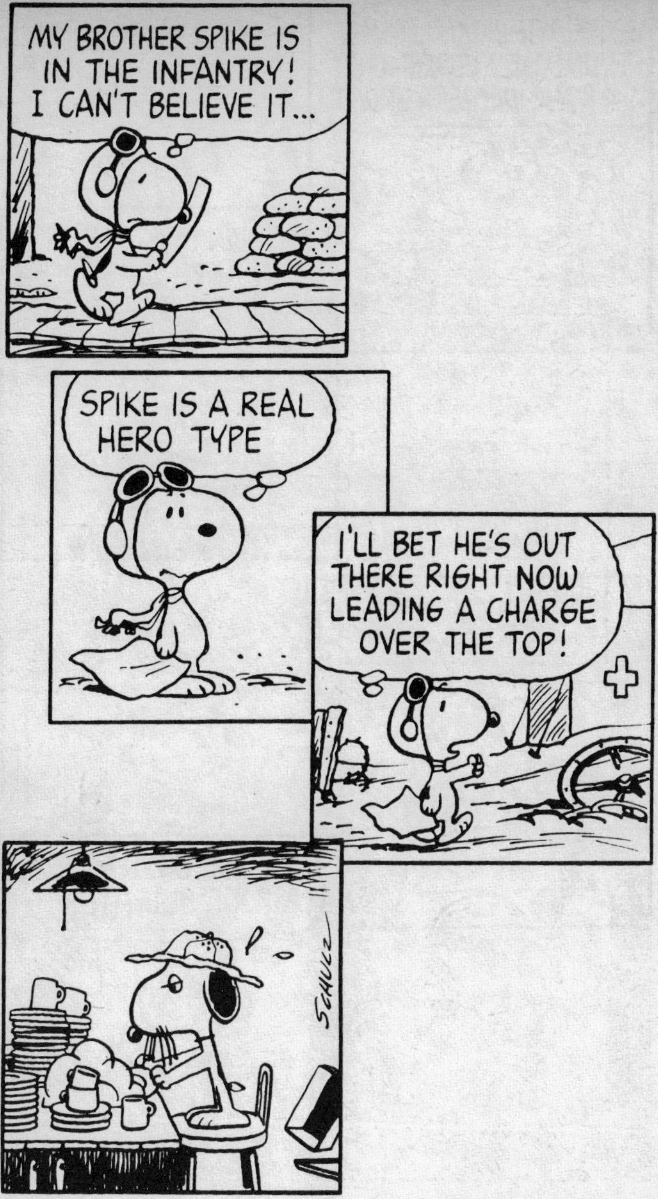
MY BROTHER SPIKE IS IN THE INFANTRY! I CAN'T BELIEVE IT...
SPIKE IS A REAL HERO TYPE
I'LL BET HE'S OUT THERE RIGHT NOW LEADING A CHARGE OVER THE TOP!
SCHULZ

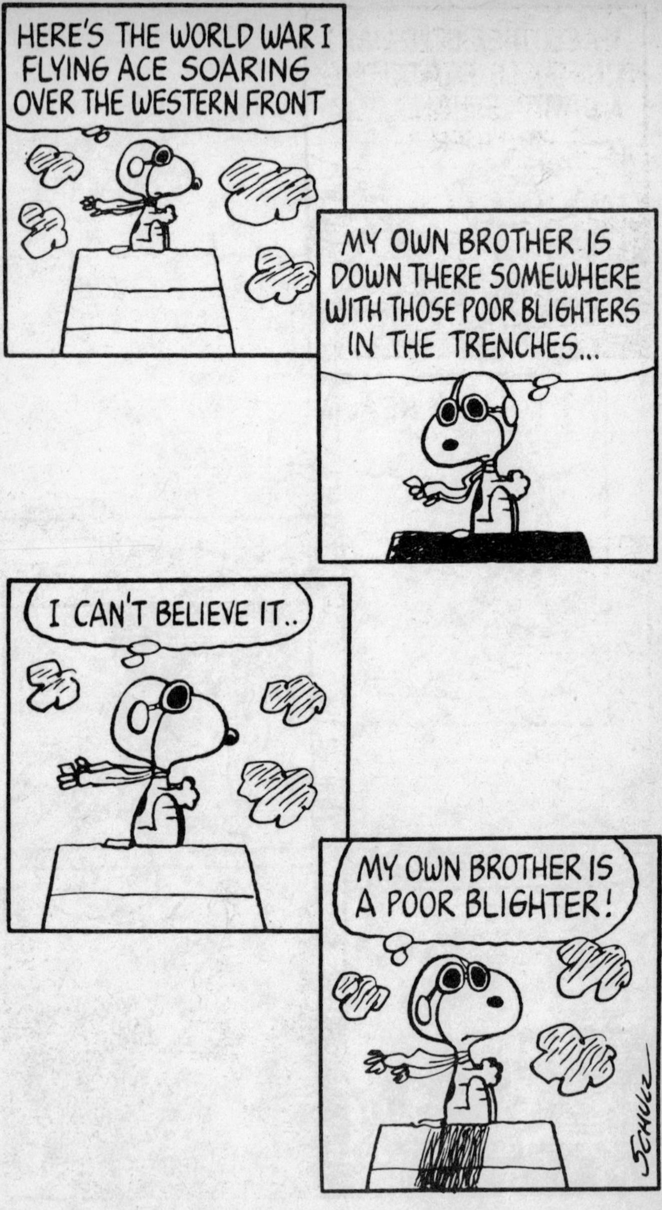
HERE'S THE WORLD WAR I FLYING ACE SOARING OVER THE WESTERN FRONT
MY OWN BROTHER IS DOWN THERE SOMEWHERE WITH THOSE POOR BLIGHTERS IN THE TRENCHES...
I CAN'T BELIEVE IT..
MY OWN BROTHER IS A POOR BLIGHTER!
SCHULZ

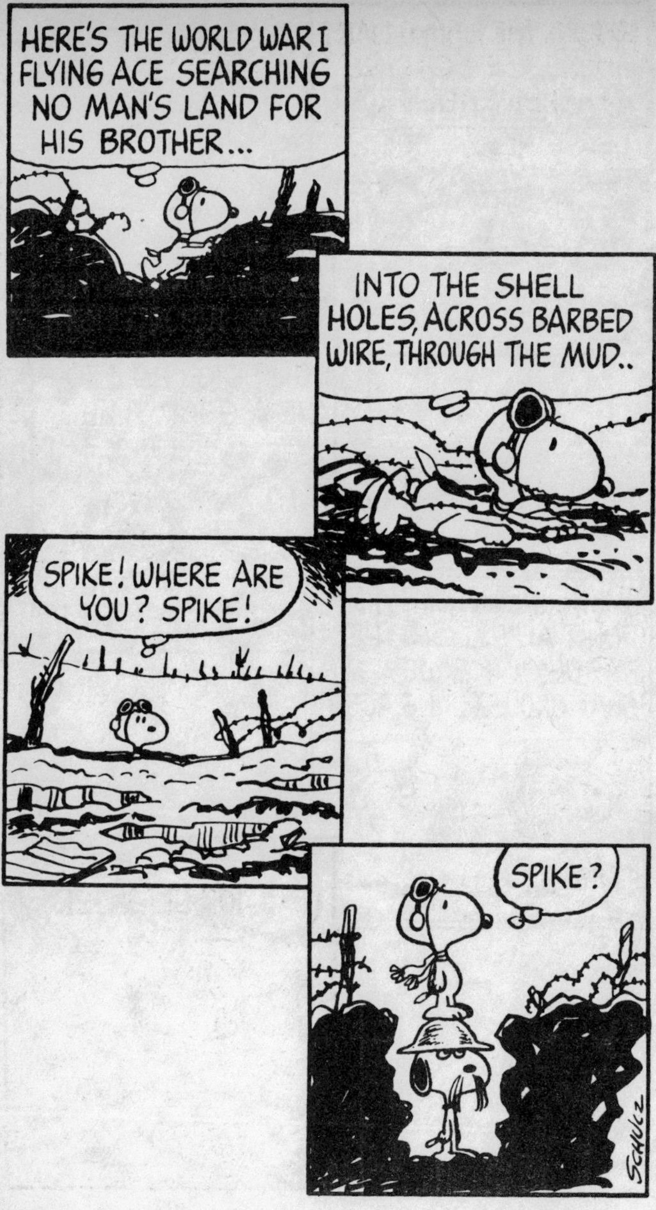
HERE'S THE WORLD WAR I FLYING ACE SEARCHING NO MAN'S LAND FOR HIS BROTHER...
INTO THE SHELL HOLES, ACROSS BARBED WIRE, THROUGH THE MUD..
SPIKE! WHERE ARE YOU? SPIKE!
SPIKE?
SCHULZ

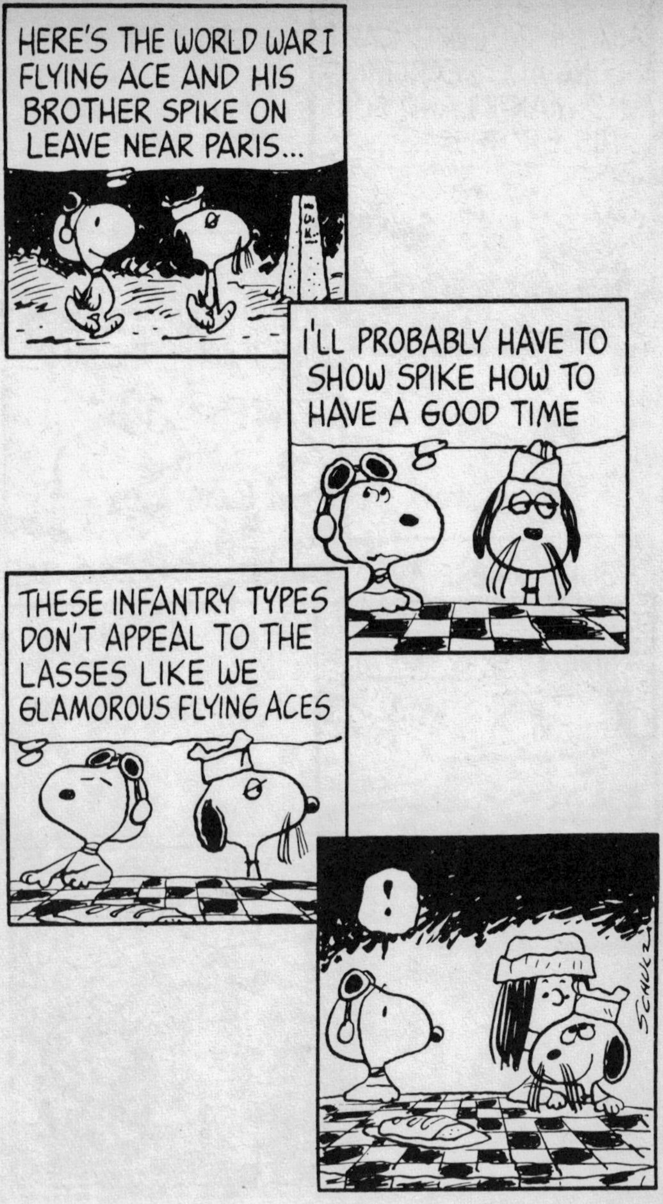
HERE'S THE WORLD WAR I FLYING ACE AND HIS BROTHER SPIKE ON LEAVE NEAR PARIS...
I'LL PROBABLY HAVE TO SHOW SPIKE HOW TO HAVE A GOOD TIME
THESE INFANTRY TYPES DON'T APPEAL TO THE LASSES LIKE WE GLAMOROUS FLYING ACES
!
SCHULZ

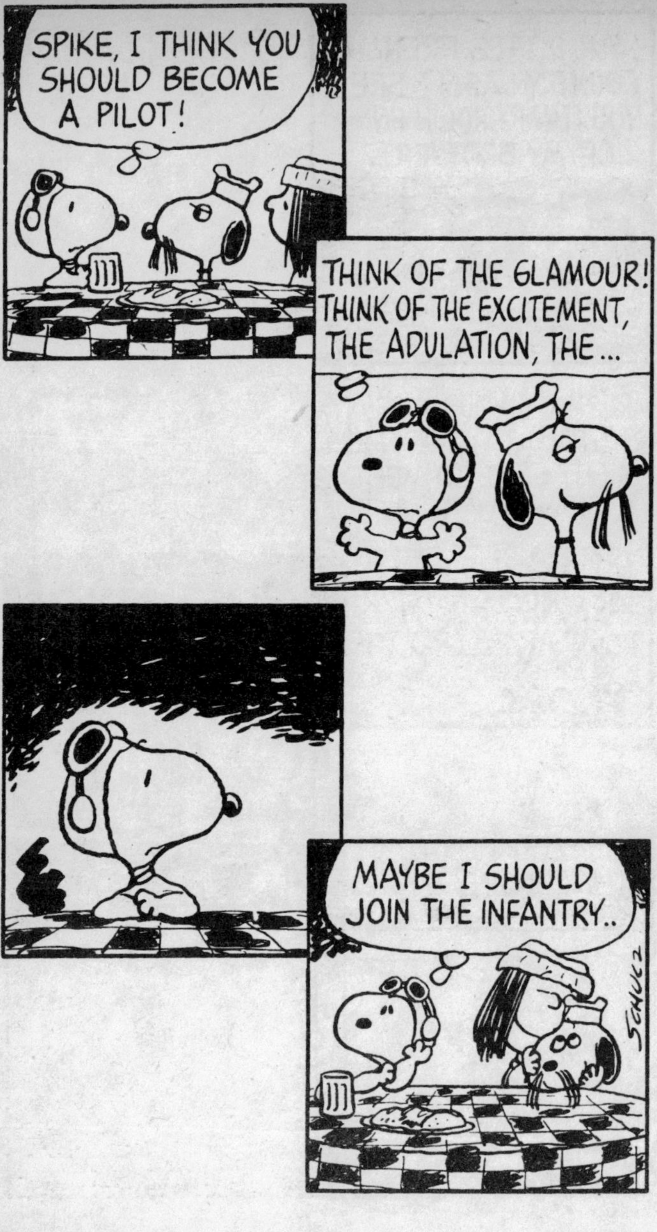
SPIKE, I THINK YOU SHOULD BECOME A PILOT!
THINK OF THE GLAMOUR! THINK OF THE EXCITEMENT, THE ADULATION, THE...
MAYBE I SHOULD JOIN THE INFANTRY..
SCHULZ

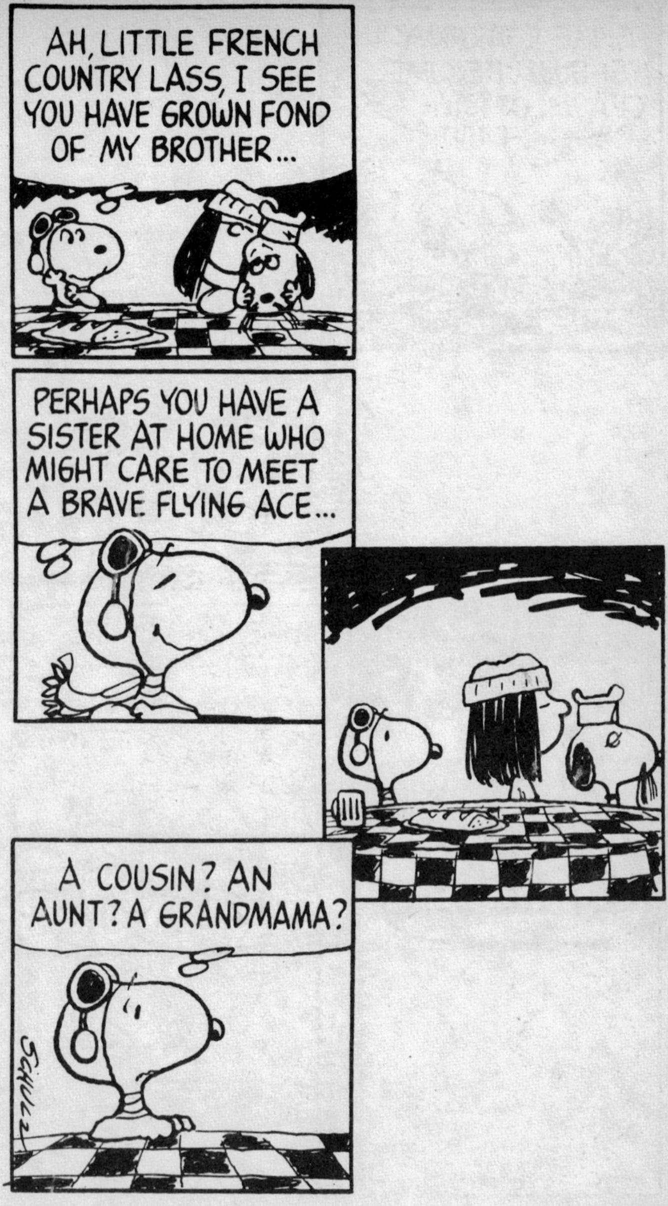

AH, LITTLE FRENCH COUNTRY LASS, I SEE YOU HAVE GROWN FOND OF MY BROTHER...
PERHAPS YOU HAVE A SISTER AT HOME WHO MIGHT CARE TO MEET A BRAVE FLYING ACE...
A COUSIN? AN AUNT? A GRANDMAMA?
SCHULZ

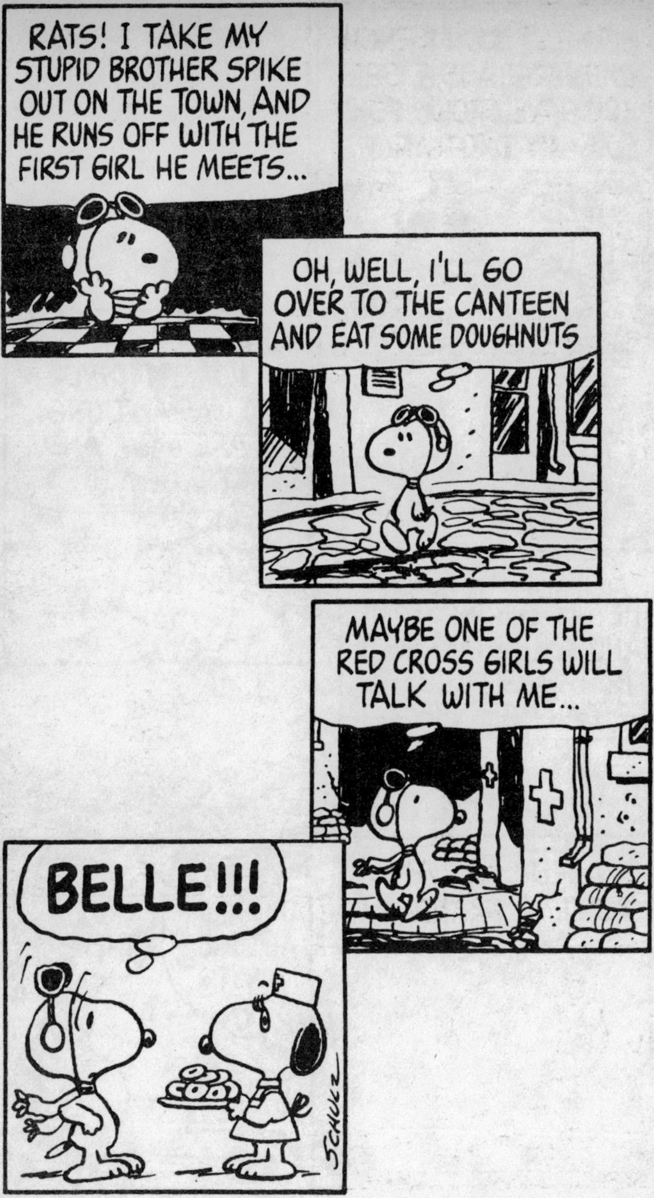

RATS! I TAKE MY STUPID BROTHER SPIKE OUT ON THE TOWN, AND HE RUNS OFF WITH THE FIRST GIRL HE MEETS...
OH, WELL, I'LL GO OVER TO THE CANTEEN AND EAT SOME DOUGHNUTS
MAYBE ONE OF THE RED CROSS GIRLS WILL TALK WITH ME...
BELLE!!!
SCHULZ

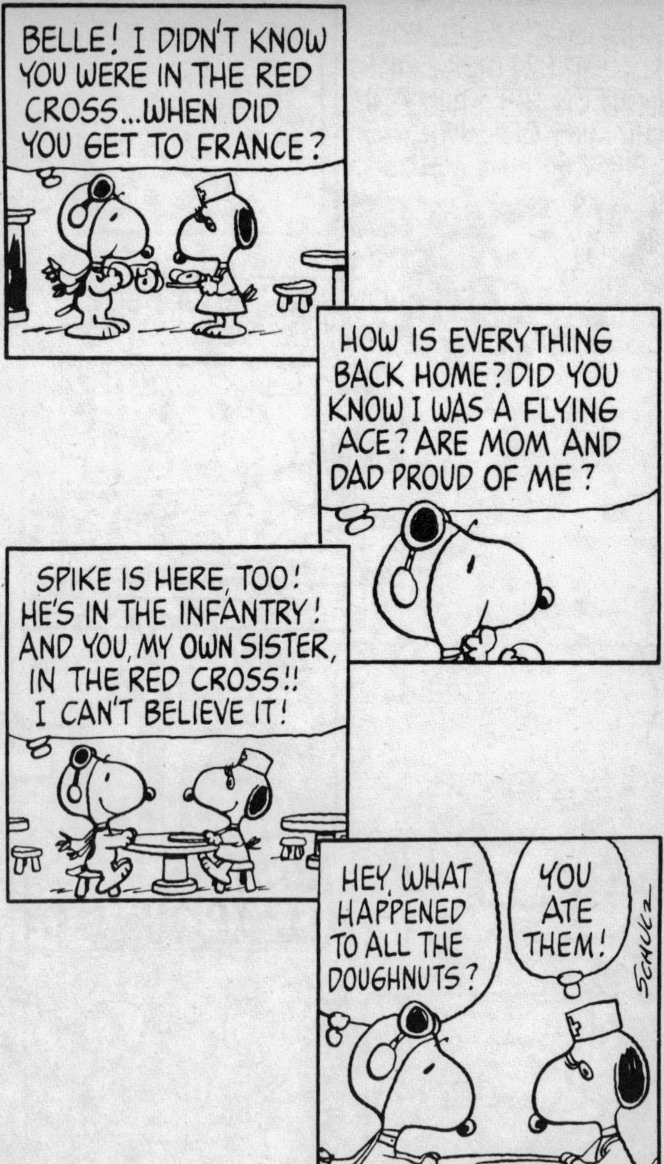
BELLE! I DIDN'T KNOW YOU WERE IN THE RED CROSS...WHEN DID YOU GET TO FRANCE?
HOW IS EVERYTHING BACK HOME? DID YOU KNOW I WAS A FLYING ACE? ARE MOM AND DAD PROUD OF ME?
SPIKE IS HERE, TOO! HE'S IN THE INFANTRY! AND YOU, MY OWN SISTER, IN THE RED CROSS!! I CAN'T BELIEVE IT!
HEY, WHAT HAPPENED TO ALL THE DOUGHNUTS?
YOU ATE THEM!
SCHULZ

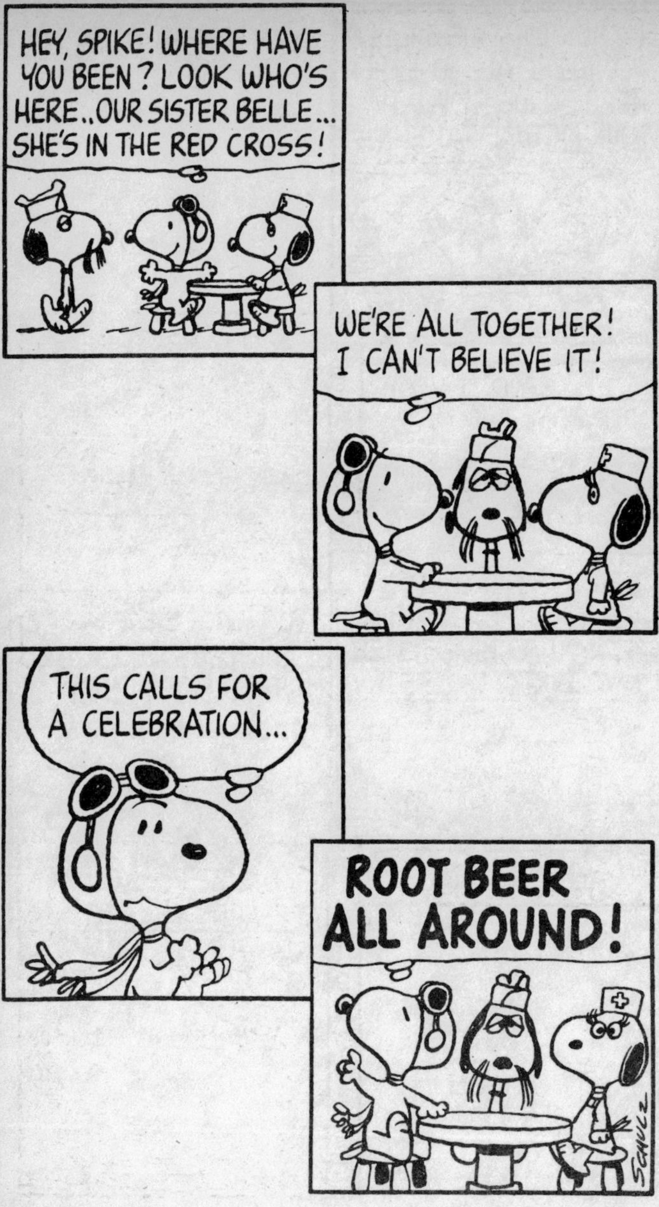
HEY, SPIKE! WHERE HAVE YOU BEEN? LOOK WHO'S HERE..OUR SISTER BELLE... SHE'S IN THE RED CROSS!
WE'RE ALL TOGETHER! I CAN'T BELIEVE IT!
THIS CALLS FOR A CELEBRATION...
ROOT BEER ALL AROUND!
SCHULZ

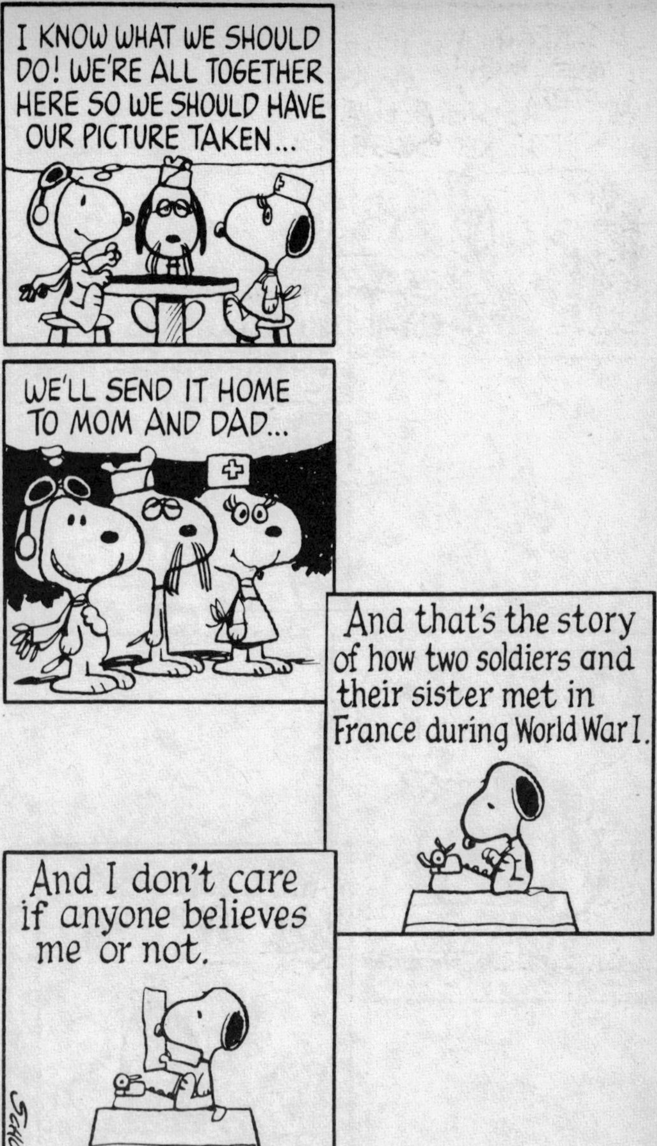
I KNOW WHAT WE SHOULD DO! WE'RE ALL TOGETHER HERE SO WE SHOULD HAVE OUR PICTURE TAKEN...
WE'LL SEND IT HOME TO MOM AND DAD...
And that's the story of how two soldiers and their sister met in France during World War I.
And I don't care if anyone believes me or not.
SCHULZ

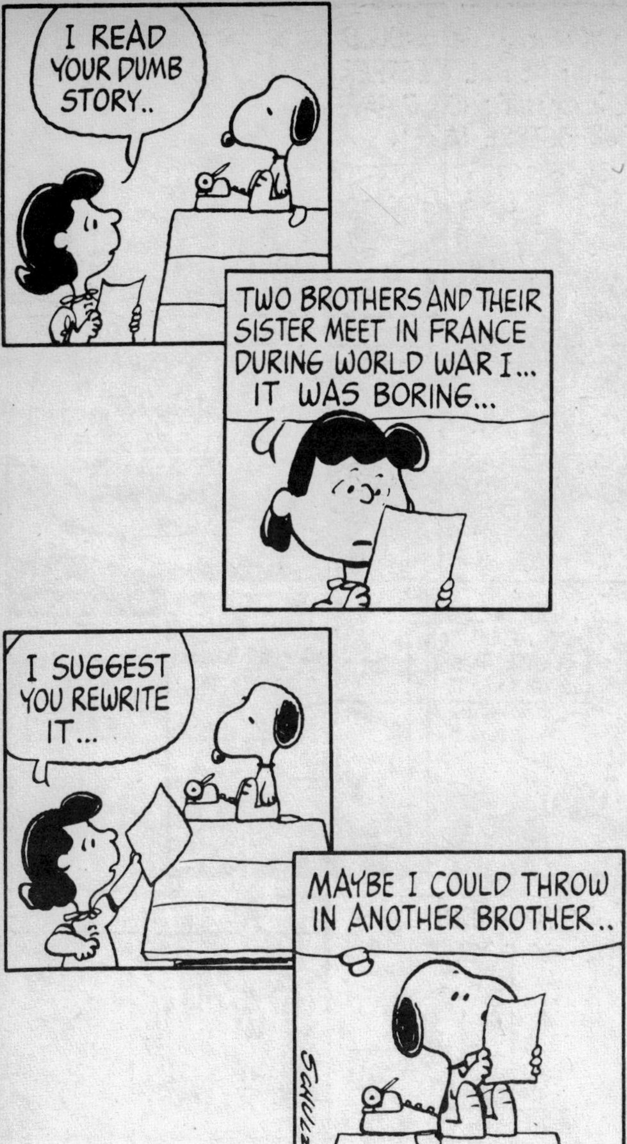
I READ YOUR DUMB STORY..
TWO BROTHERS AND THEIR SISTER MEET IN FRANCE DURING WORLD WAR I... IT WAS BORING...
I SUGGEST YOU REWRITE IT...
MAYBE I COULD THROW IN ANOTHER BROTHER..
SCHULZ

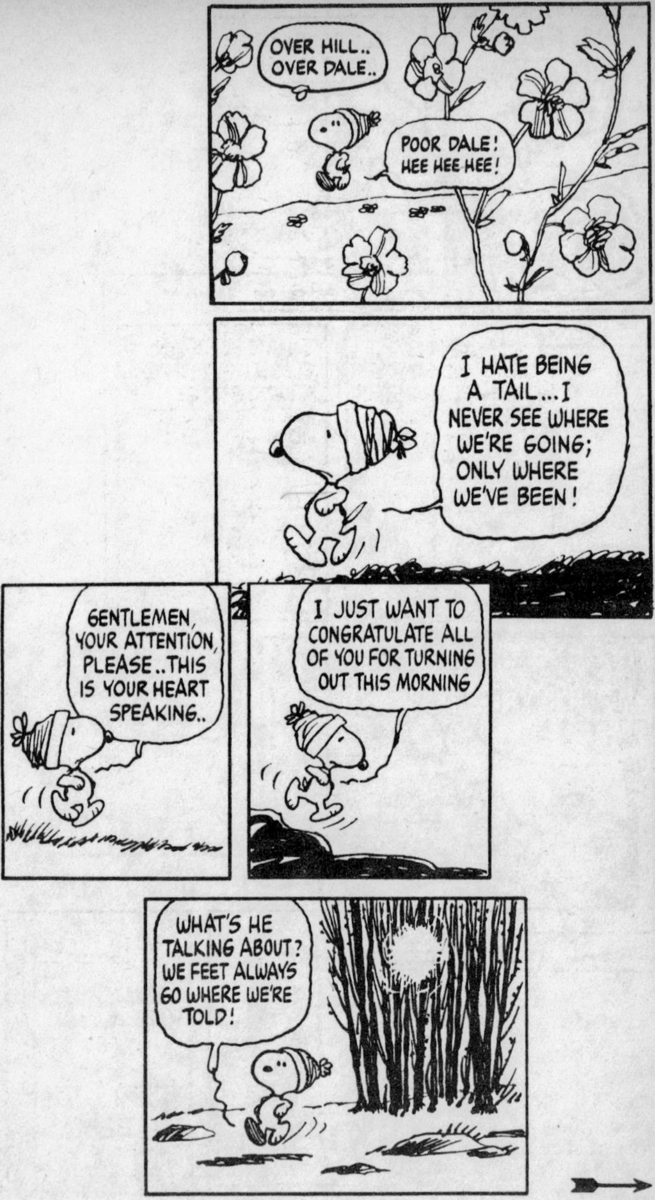
OVER HILL.. OVER DALE..
POOR DALE! HEE HEE HEE!
I HATE BEING A TAIL...I NEVER SEE WHERE WE'RE GOING; ONLY WHERE WE'VE BEEN!
GENTLEMEN, YOUR ATTENTION, PLEASE..THIS IS YOUR HEART SPEAKING..
I JUST WANT TO CONGRATULATE ALL OF YOU FOR TURNING OUT THIS MORNING
WHAT'S HE TALKING ABOUT? WE FEET ALWAYS GO WHERE WE'RE TOLD!

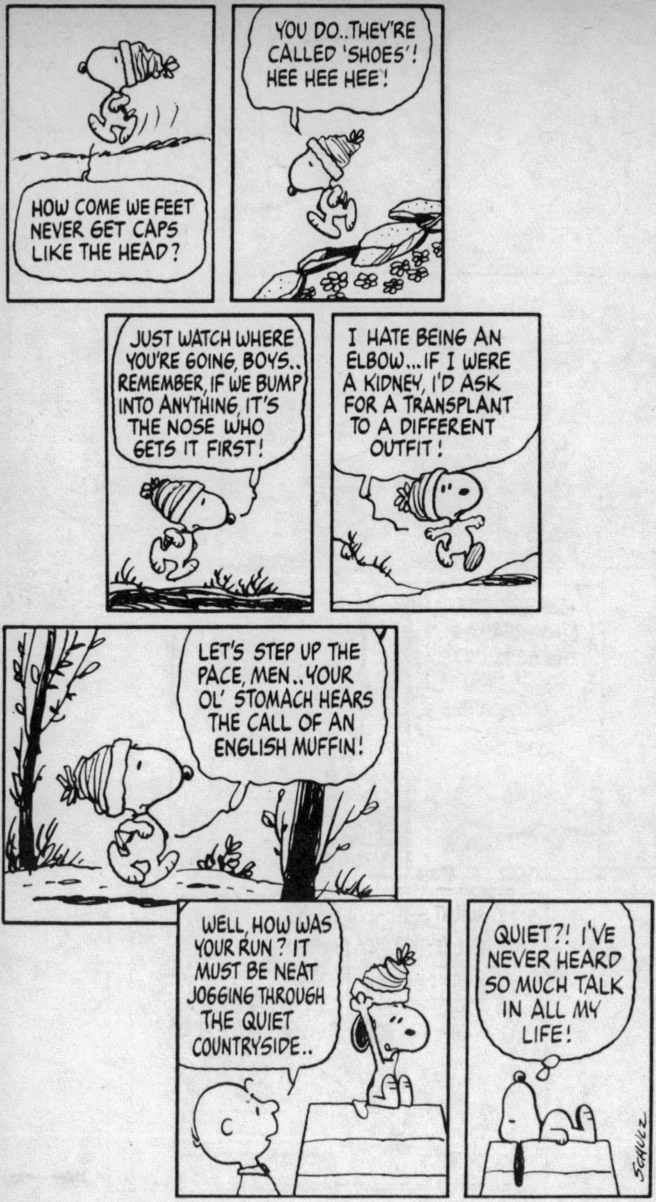
HOW COME WE FEET NEVER GET CAPS LIKE THE HEAD?
YOU DO..THEY'RE CALLED 'SHOES'! HEE HEE HEE!
JUST WATCH WHERE YOU'RE GOING, BOYS.. REMEMBER, IF WE BUMP INTO ANYTHING, IT'S THE NOSE WHO GETS IT FIRST!
I HATE BEING AN ELBOW...IF I WERE A KIDNEY, I'D ASK FOR A TRANSPLANT TO A DIFFERENT OUTFIT!
LET'S STEP UP THE PACE, MEN..YOUR OL' STOMACH HEARS THE CALL OF AN ENGLISH MUFFIN!
WELL, HOW WAS YOUR RUN? IT MUST BE NEAT JOGGING THROUGH THE QUIET COUNTRYSIDE..
QUIET?! I'VE NEVER HEARD SO MUCH TALK IN ALL MY LIFE!
SCHULZ

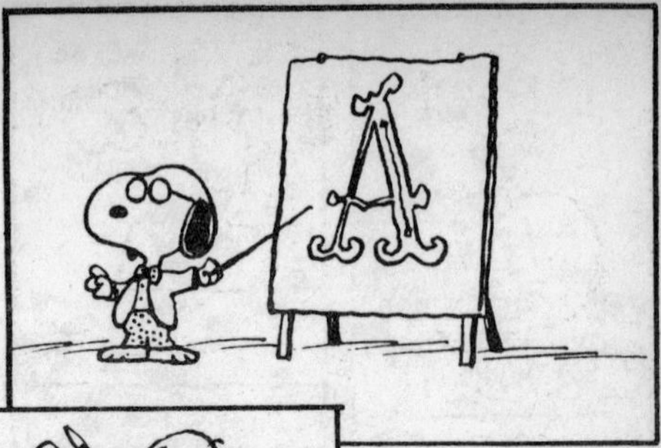

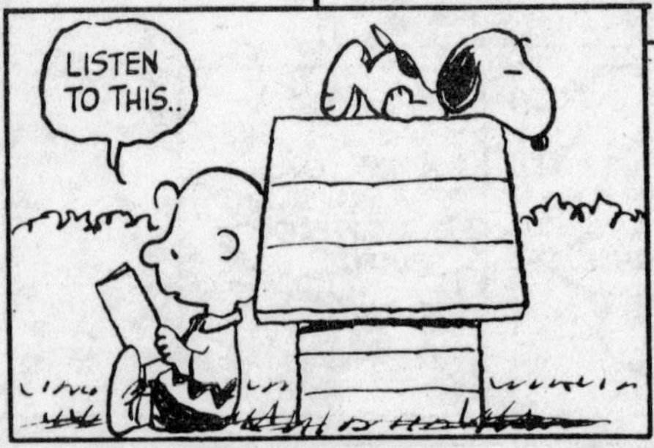
LISTEN TO THIS..

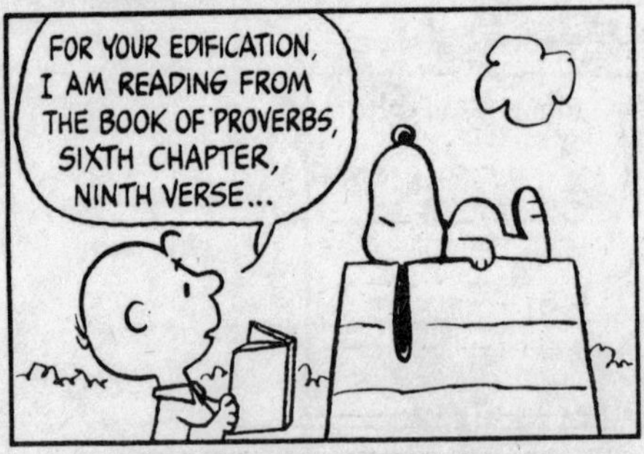
FOR YOUR EDIFICATION, I AM READING FROM THE BOOK OF PROVERBS, SIXTH CHAPTER, NINTH VERSE...

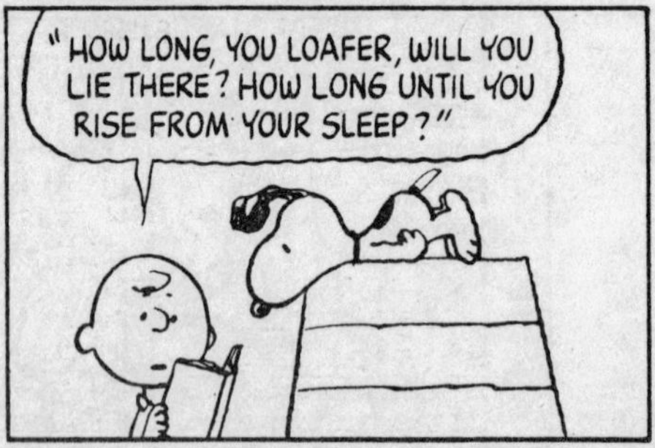
"HOW LONG, YOU LOAFER, WILL YOU LIE THERE? HOW LONG UNTIL YOU RISE FROM YOUR SLEEP?"

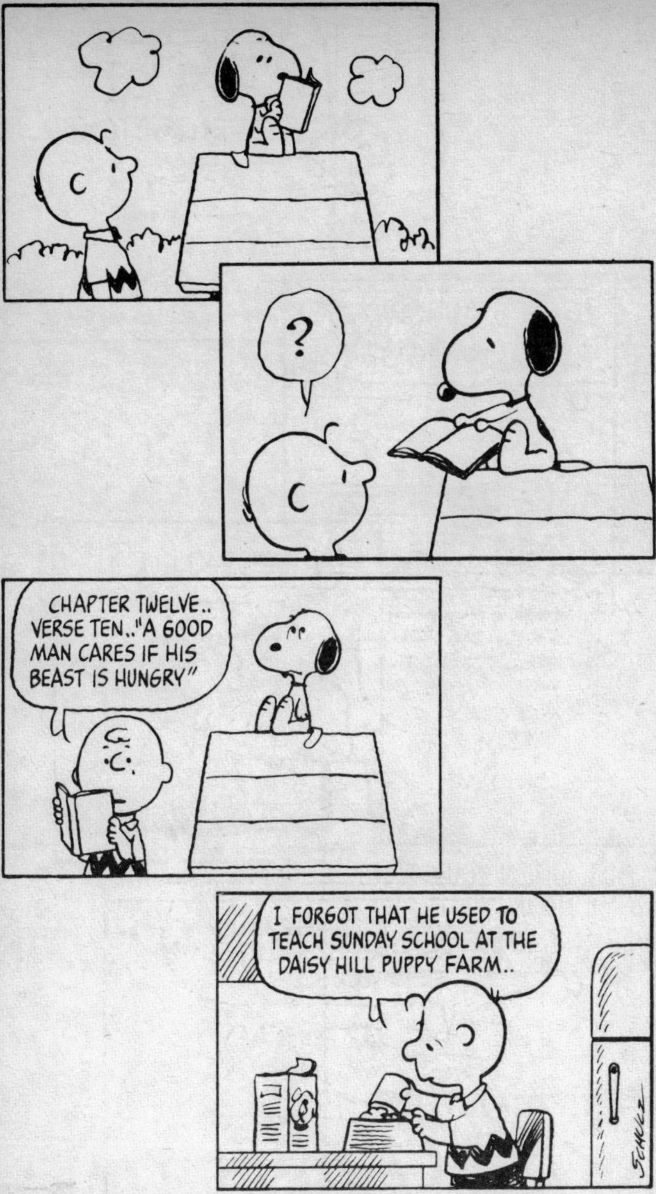
?
CHAPTER TWELVE.. VERSE TEN.."A GOOD MAN CARES IF HIS BEAST IS HUNGRY"
I FORGOT THAT HE USED TO TEACH SUNDAY SCHOOL AT THE DAISY HILL PUPPY FARM..
SCHULZ

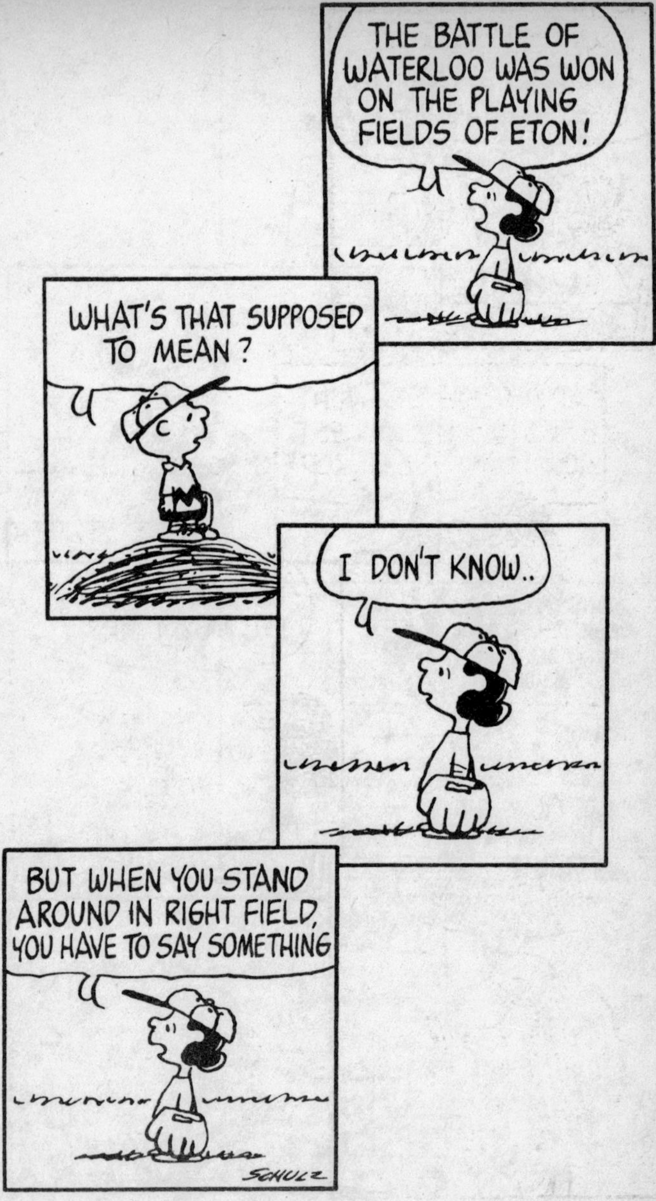
THE BATTLE OF WATERLOO WAS WON ON THE PLAYING FIELDS OF ETON!
WHAT'S THAT SUPPOSED TO MEAN?
I DON'T KNOW..
BUT WHEN YOU STAND AROUND IN RIGHT FIELD, YOU HAVE TO SAY SOMETHING
SCHULZ

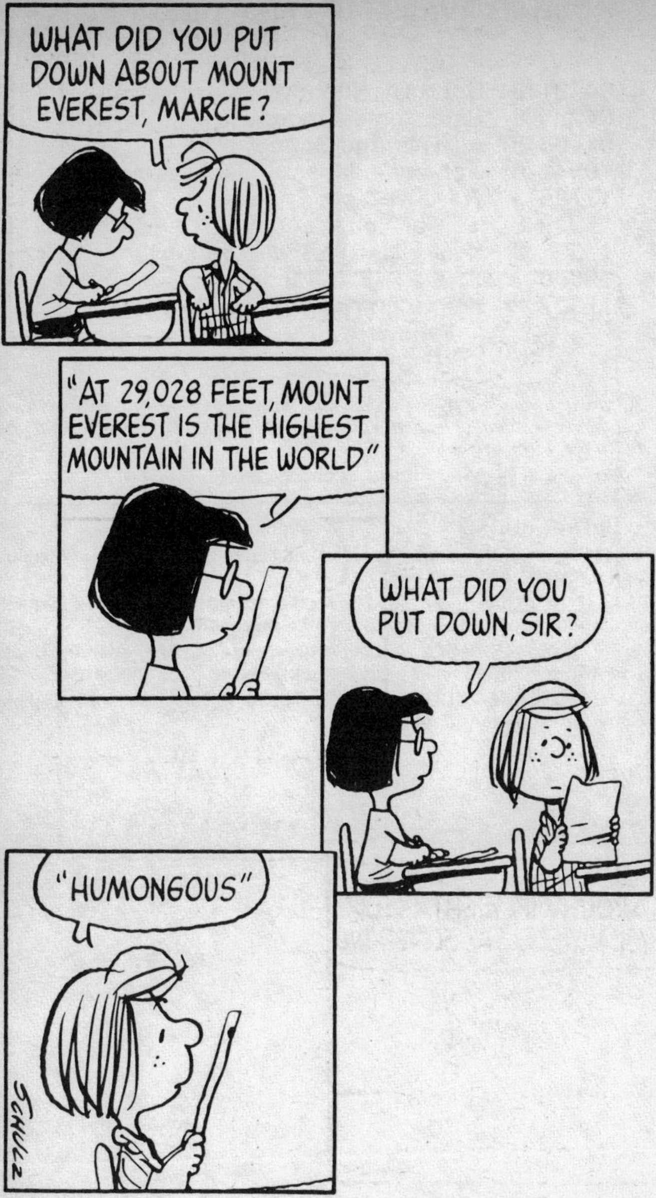
WHAT DID YOU PUT DOWN ABOUT MOUNT EVEREST, MARCIE?
"AT 29,028 FEET, MOUNT EVEREST IS THE HIGHEST MOUNTAIN IN THE WORLD"
WHAT DID YOU PUT DOWN, SIR?
"HUMONGOUS"
SCHULZ

ALSO AVAILABLE FROM CORONET

All these books are available at your local bookshop or newsagent, or can be ordered direct from the publisher. Just tick the titles you want and fill in the form below.

Prices and availability subject to change without notice.

CORONET BOOKS, P.O. Box 11, Falmouth, Cornwall.

Please send cheque or postal order, and allow the following for postage and packing:

U.K. – 50p for one book, plus 20p for the second book, and 14p for each additional book ordered up to a £1.68 maximum.

B.F.P.O. and EIRE – 50p for the first book, plus 20p for the second book, and 14p per copy for the next 7 books, 8p per book thereafter.

OTHER OVERSEAS CUSTOMERS – 75p for the first book, plus 21p per copy for each additional book.

Name ....

Address..

....